CH00894060

WHEN THE WAR CAME TO SEIGHFORD

The story of an RAF airfield

Bruce Braithwaite

Best Wishes

Bruce Braithwaite

BRULA BOOKS

© Bruce Braithwaite 2007
When the War came to Seighford

ISBN : 978-0-9557645-0-9

Published by:
Brula Books
29 Thames Way
Western Downs
Stafford
ST17 9AZ

Designed by Michael Walsh at
The Better Book Company
A division of
RPM Print & Design
2-3 Spur Road
Chichester
West Sussex
PO19 8PR

CONTENTS

Introduction i

1   From farm field to airfield..............................1

2   30 Operational Training Unit 9

3   The first year 19

4   Memories of an air gunner 29

5   More losses...39

6   Tragedy over Cannock Chase 49

7   Aftermath of Arnhem 57

8   'The sky was full of Oxfords' 66

9   Life on the farm.......................................77

10 Ground work..83

11 Ready for the enemy...............................90

12 Off duty..98

13 After the war 105

14 Commemoration 111

    Acknowledgements.................................118

    Bibliography 119

INTRODUCTION

R AF Seighford was just one of fifteen World War II airfields in Staffordshire but it does have its own special story. Over sixty years have elapsed since it became operational in September 1942. Now Seighford's relics are disappearing with each passing year. One day there might be no trace of the airfield left – except the memories.

In telling the wartime history of the site I also try to give an impression of those RAF years. An impression gained mainly from the thoughts of thirty people; ex-service personnel or local villagers who were there. The story is told as often as possible in their words – these are the italics which appear throughout the book.

During my research I heard about many incidents – some exciting, some hilarious and, alas, some tragic; I met many interesting, helpful and hospitable people; I was privileged to become a member of the airfield's 50th anniversary committee. The reality of the story finally hit home however when I stood at the graveside of several young men whose last flight was from a Seighford runway.

Hundreds of men and women – members of the Royal Air Force, the Royal Australian Air Force, the Royal Canadian Air Force, the Royal New Zealand Air Force, the Women's Auxiliary Air Force, and civilians – served at Seighford.

THIS BOOK IS DEDICATED TO THEM

i

1

FROM FARM FIELD TO AIRFIELD

Seighford hasn't changed too much over the past seventy years. It is easy to picture it as it was in the late-1930s with the main road winding between St Chad's church and the school, and past those other essential elements of village life, the pub and the shop. Around the village lay the farmland crossed by a network of west Staffordshire country lanes.

How picturesque it looked in springtime and the summer. The countryside round here was full of beautiful flowers. The frontage of Seighford Hall used to be thick with daffodils. Even William's Wood was full of anemones.

Grange Lane was beautiful, especially when the primroses were out in spring.

That was the pastoral Seighford scene in the summer of 1939. No-one knew then that it would be the last summer of peace for six years, or that those pleasant views with their beautiful flowers would never be quite the same again.

September brought the start of World War II. The village school's logbook duly recorded:

11th September 1939 – the staff attended school to make arrangements for re-opening, which had been postponed from 4th September because of the outbreak of war.

Later entries reflected how serious the situation had become:

5th October 1939 – a member of the Architect's Department visited to enquire about the provision of an air raid shelter for the school.

14th May 1940 – school re-opened this morning by order of the Government because of the German invasion of Holland

and Belgium. The remainder of the Whitsuntide Holiday has been cancelled.

21st October 1940 – the warning system this morning necessitated taking shelter at the vicarage from 10.30 until 11.40 a.m.

It was not long before an even more drastic effect on life in Seighford began. The Midlands was becoming a vast Royal Air Force training ground for the thousands of new aircrew needed for the counter-offensive against Germany and the rest of Nazi-occupied Europe. New airfields mushroomed across the area when the Air Ministry assessed the number of bomber training units it required to meet the heavy demand for aircrew. Staffordshire, like other central counties, came under close scrutiny. Surveyors scoured the countryside seeking suitable sites and Seighford's potential was soon recognised.

Four hundred and eighty acres of the relatively flat expanse of land, four or five miles west of the town of Stafford, were requisitioned by the Air Ministry. Compensation was paid to the owners, the Eld estate, at two guineas (£2-10p) per acre. Most of the required land belonged to Hextall Farm, and more came from the adjoining farms of Clanford Hall and the Grange. The three properties were farmed by brothers Frederick and Frank Parrott.

The main area for the new aerodrome extended from Five Lane Ends in the west to the grounds of Seighford Hall in the east, and south to the farmyard of Clanford Hall. The Woodseaves-Great Bridgeford road formed a ready-made northern boundary for the actual airfield. This stretch of road would remain open to the public throughout the war. At least it was usually open – there were several occasions when it was blocked by an aircraft that had overshot the end of the main runway and crunched to a halt astride the highway. *There was even one incident when a Wellington bomber was coming in to land too low and its wheels clipped the roof of a double-decker bus passing along the road.*

After a preliminary check by the Ministry in February 1941, a full survey of the site was carried out in late April-early May, and construction work began in June. The main contractor for RAF Seighford was Sir Lindsay Parkinson & Company, who carried out many such projects during the war. The contract was valued at £750,000 (equivalent to well over £20 million today) and the work took just over a year to complete.

The Air Ministry site plans reveal the extent of the military aerodrome and its impact on the Seighford landscape. Although the main focus was the actual airfield, there were more than 320 buildings and other features making up the RAF establishment. It was built as a fully operational bomber station – the aircraft dispersal areas even had anchor blocks for Short Stirlings, the RAF's first four-engine heavy bomber.

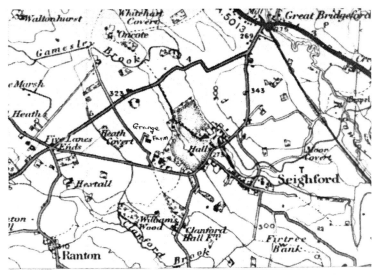

The rural scene at Seighford before the RAF arrived (Reproduced from the 1920 Ordnance Survey Map)

3

The workforce consisted of about one thousand men at the peak of the project. Most of them moved from contract to contract, and several hundred were accommodated in a 'labour camp' on what was to become the service personnel's living quarters. Other construction workers travelled to the site on private buses hired from Stafford and the surrounding district.

The site was a big employer of local labour. Many local youths were employed in the airfield construction before they went into the Forces.

One personnel problem was the shortage of competent drivers for the site's seventy or so lorries and dumpers as most of the suitable men were already on war service. This led to problems with the police over motoring offences but none were of a serious nature.

In fact there was little to upset the local constabulary. *Even with all that amount of young men building or serving at the airfield, there was never any serious trouble; never any burglary or rape.*

∗   ∗   ∗

Seighford village was seldom visited by anyone from the site, mainly due to the fact that the Holly Bush pub would not serve them. This is understandable as it would have been crowded out by site labour. It was only a small Parkers Brewery house and landlord Bromley fetched drinks in a jug from a beer barrel in the cellar.

∗   ∗   ∗

The local shop for the construction force was the village store in Great Bridgeford. This had a popular speciality: home-made parkin toffee, a luxury in those days of food rationing.

4

The project began with the clearance of the site, especially any obstruction that would endanger the aircraft. Two houses and five or six smaller buildings had to be demolished. Luckily this did not involve the impressive 16th-century half-timbered Seighford Hall, or the equally picturesque Clanford Hall which would be even nearer to a runway.

The buildings of Grange Farm, however, lay right on the planned airfield. *The farmhouse, buildings and cottages were completely demolished. It was red brick-built house, quite old – possibly 200 years. Before it was demolished it was measured inch by inch with the promise that it would be rebuilt after the war.* Sadly, nothing came of this assurance and the house did not rise again once the hostilities were over. One of the outbuildings did have a temporary reprieve while it was used as a site canteen for the construction workers.

Two other casualties of the clearance were Grange Lane with its beautiful flowers, and the road that ran direct from Five Lane Ends to Seighford village. The latter road was *dead straight; so straight I looked at it almost in awe as a young boy.* Both it and Grange Lane crossed the site of the airfield and so had to be erased from the landscape.

The pre-war Seighford countryside was quite heavily wooded; many trees on and around the airfield had to be felled.

We lived near a big pit that was surrounded by trees. As this lay in the flightpath for the main runway, the trees were cut down by fellers with great double-headed axes. It provided us with logs for months.

✳   ✳   ✳

Some of the trees were cut down by the local farmers. They were allocated a supply of fence posts in return.

✳   ✳   ✳

The tree stumps also had to be removed. Large ones in the

central part of the airfield were blasted out by a specialist explosives firm. Those by the main road at the Ellenhall end were pulled out by a steam engine. Chains from the engine winched them out like pulling rotten teeth.

The next major task was the levelling of the ground. Most of this was done by a specialist sub-contractor, En-tout-cas Limited, a firm well known before and after the war for the much smaller job of laying tennis courts. *The areas between the runways were levelled by scrapers pulled by bulldozers. Not many drivers were available for this work so they had to work practically all the hours of daylight in the summer of 1942.*

❖ ❖ ❖

We lived at Bridgeford and had lodgers during the war. The first two were En-tout-cas drivers by the name of Scott and Pratt. Pratt weighed about eighteen stone and came from Stockport. I was only a schoolboy at the time and he let me ride on his bulldozer.

Other workmen remembered by local people were the gangs of Irishmen who dug the trenches for the new water mains. *They got the blame if anything went missing. Two bikes disappeared from the shed behind our house but nothing was ever proved.*

❖ ❖ ❖

The labourers were even blamed for digging up all the daffodils in front of Seighford Hall.

The levelling work encountered a few problems. A stream near Heath Covert had to be piped underground. And there were all the ponds and pits dotting the farm fields. The holes were often filled with felled tree trunks, and at least two of them received 'retired' bulldozers. One pit on Hextall Farm, thirty feet deep, claimed a dumper that fell in accidentally and had to be abandoned.

The concreting of the runways, perimeter-tracks and hardstandings was the main operation of the construction programme. Convoys of lorries brought sand and gravel from quarries near Brocton. They also collected aggregate from Woodseaves, and Welsh granite chippings that had been delivered to the railway station at Great Bridgeford. The concrete was mixed at a batching plant located near the centre of the site, and transported to where it was needed by a diesel locomotive running along a narrow-gauge railway track. About three miles of this track were laid; some of it was still being unearthed fifty years later when the fields were ploughed. The farmer was mystified to find traces of a railway on his land until he learned about the wartime concrete-carrying transport system.

The locomotive was supplemented by a 'Rex Paver', *an American machine rare in this country.* This mixed concrete and laid it via a hopper on a boom. Being mobile and having a high output, the paver proved to be a vital piece of equipment in the airfield's construction.

All the labour on the contract were paid under the Government's 'payment by results' scheme – which meant that everyone was interested in achieving the maximum possible output.

The winter of 1941-42 was especially cold and caused problems with the concrete laying. Although special additives were used to combat the low temperatures, some areas had to be hacked up and re-laid. Fortunately the following summer was a good one and time was made up.

Some doubt still crops up about the original length of the main runway at Seighford. The confusion is due to the apparent extension beyond the lane linking Seighford village with Coton Clanford. The Air Ministry's regulation length for a main runway when the site was first proposed was 1,600 yards. This requirement was changed to 2,000 yards in October 1941 i.e. while the construction work was underway. *All the runways were lengthened from the original conception – the main one by extending beyond the perimeter-track.*

No attempt was made to lengthen the perimeter-track to reach the 'new' end of the main runway. So Seighford always had its regulation 2,000-yard runway – a fact verified by the residents of Clanford Hall who experienced the difficulties of having to cross it when travelling along the lane.

The construction of Seighford's RAF station took just over twelve months. There was one delay in building when the Ministry sent posters about German atrocities to 'gee-up' the workforce. An accompanying letter stated that the posters were designed for 'low intelligence' workers. This letter was seen by workers who were so insulted by it that they went on strike.

Another setback happened early in 1942 when the site offices were destroyed by fire. The nearby armoury was almost finished by that time and was able to be used as temporary office accommodation.

All problems were overcome and RAF Seighford became operational on 16 September 1942. *The tarmac was hardly dry when the first Wellingtons landed.*

2

30 OPERATIONAL TRAINING UNIT

No.30 Operational Training Unit began life on 28 June 1942. As part of 93 (OTU) Group Bomber Command, its duty was *to take trained pilots, navigators, bomb aimers, wireless operators and air gunners and form them into bomber crews before transferring them to a Heavy Conversion Unit where they would be given a short course in flying larger bombers such as the Lancaster and Halifax. From the Heavy Conversion Unit the crews would be posted to operational squadrons.*

RAF Seighford was built as a fully operational bomber station. It was only when the construction work was finished that the airfield was given a training role and became part of 30 OTU. The Unit's first, and main, base was RAF Hixon, four miles north-east of Stafford. With all respect, Hixon seems a slightly unlikely location for a bomber airfield. It was situated in an angle created by the junction of the London, Midland & Scottish Railway line and the smaller Stafford & Uttoxeter Railway. Some runways ended a mere two hundred feet from these railway lines.

It was said that Seighford should have been the parent airfield as aircraft very often overshot the runway at Hixon and ended up on the railway line. There was panic to get them off as there was the possibility of a train approaching. There was a prime example on 1 August 1943 when a Wellington bomber had to land without flaps after losing its hydraulics. The resulting high speed carried the aircraft down the runway and onto the railway line where it caught fire.

Another limitation was the fact that Hixon's main runway was only 1,580 yards long. *It was not long enough for aircraft fully loaded with 4,000 lbs of bombs to take off. So they came over to Seighford to be loaded.*

And the weather was said to be often better at Seighford. *It did not have much trouble with weather conditions and remained open when Hixon was closed for days on end.*

Seighford did have one potential obstacle however. Two and a half miles away but only fifteen degrees off the alignment of the main runway, the twin towers of Stafford Castle rose sixty feet above the landscape. The castle was a good landmark by day but a hazard by night. Happily no aircraft collided with the historic building – to the great relief of the Home Guard unit occupying a lookout post on top of one of the towers.

There were official landmarks for the aircraft – every RAF airfield had its own two-letter identification code. Seighford was 'YD' and *these letters, well over ten feet high, were propped up at the end of the airfield and illuminated at night.*

The workhorse of the operational training units was the twin-engine Vickers Wellington medium bomber. The RAF had a nickname for this aircraft – the 'Wimpy', so called after a popular character in the Popeye cartoon strip: J Wellington Wimpy.

The majority of the Wimpys at 30 OTU and other training units had already been put through a full working life. *These aircraft were usually hand-me-downs from frontline squadrons and needed considerable attention. Many were kept flying long after they should have been grounded.*

The trainee crews were worked pretty hard at their OTU. With an average age not much more than twenty, they came from all parts of Britain and, what was still in those days, the Empire. They were selected for their particular aptitudes and received specialised basic training. Once qualified in their own 'trade', the young men came together at an OTU to form a crew and learn to fly together.

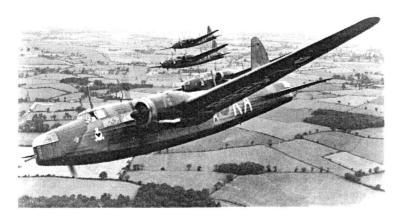

workhorse of 30 OTU, the Vickers Wellington

The selection process to form an individual crew was extremely simple. A number of newly qualified pilots were taken to a large room, often a hangar, where they were joined by a similar number of equally newly qualified navigators, wireless operators, bomb aimers and air gunners. They were then left to mill around and form themselves into five-man crews by some means of natural selection. This random system worked surprisingly well in the vast majority of cases. The crew usually kept the same members, apart from enforced changes due to injury or illness, throughout their training and subsequent service with the bomber squadrons.

I was an Air Gunner and crewed up with an all-sergeants crew. The Skipper was Bill 'Red' Sullock from Bristol, Navigator Stan Hanns RCAF (called 'Dad', being the oldest amongst us), Bomb Aimer Jim Barber RCAF, and Wireless Operator/ Air Gunner Bill Davies from Lancashire (a whizz-kid on the wireless and Morse key).

The Unit's instructors were experienced men who had already completed a full tour of bombing missions, usually thirty, and were 'screened' from squadron duty by a posting to an OTU. This 'rest' from operations while they passed on their knowledge and wisdom could be almost as dangerous for the instructors as flying with a squadron. *The state of the Wellingtons combined with the youthful inexperience of the crews meant that the number of fatal accidents during training was high. Some courses lost 25% of their strength.* Quite often there was a screened instructor on board on these fatal flights and he perished with his pupils. It was a cruel irony – *some of the aircrew instructors had got through two tours of ops, which was a miracle in 1942-43.*

Flight Lieutenant Steve Boylan arrived at Hixon in November 1942 having completed a tour in Wimpys (the survival rate on a Wellington squadron at that time was about 10%). He then served at 30 OTU as a flying instructor for seventeen months. *As the senior pilot instructors, we formed our own 'flying circus' and alternated duties between Hixon and Seighford as we trained the new pilots in take-off & landing, and general familiarisation with the aircraft.*

Flying Officer Walter Carter of the Royal New Zealand Air Force, having completed his tour of ops, was stationed at

Screened navigation instructors at Seighford, 1943
Flying Officer Walter Carter is second from the left

Seighford from April to October 1943 as Navigation Leader of 'D' Flight. *One of the characters on our navigation instruction team was Flying Officer 'Wild Bill' Hickox. He used to wear the 'Flying Boot' emblem on his uniform which signified someone who had walked back to base from a downed aircraft while serving on ops in North Africa.*

Transforming the individual trainees into a Wellington crew meant them flying together through a variety of tasks until they were fully proficient – then they learned to do it all over again by night.

Flying training began with the very basics. The plane took off, flew round to the other end of the runway and landed. The procedure, listed officially as 'circuits & landings', was for the obvious reason better known as 'circuits & bumps'.

I'll never forget the first circuit & bump made by our skipper. After much help from the instructor, he landed the Wellington on its tail wheel – from about twenty feet up!

Once the pilot was competent in getting the plane up and down safely, training progressed to flights away from the airfield. The journeys got longer; *cross-country flights could last up to six and a half hours and have two or three instructors on board for navigation and gunnery exercises. A typical route was over to the Isle of Man, up the Scottish coast and back down via Cumberland to Lake Vrynwy in Wales, and home via a visit to a practice bombing range such as the one on Cannock Chase.*

Some aircraft did not return from these long-distance flights. Wellington BJ801 left Hixon on 6 June 1943 for a navigation exercise which included gunnery practice over the North Sea. The plane and its crew were never seen again.

The aiming point on the Cannock Chase bombing range, just to the west of the Sherbrook Valley, was a brick-built obelisk standing a few feet high. It was painted yellow and made even more visible for the bomber crews by being surrounded by a wide circle of broken pieces of white ceramic washbasins and toilet bowls. *There were usually two Wellingtons at a time flying along the Cannock Chase range. Some would drop flares to illuminate the target then release their bombs.* These visits were not particularly popular with the Forestry Commission workers as they had to be on standby to put out any fires created by the 'raids'. Other inhabitants of the neighbourhood may also have been worried – *some of the practice bombs dropped on the Cannock Chase range were found well off target – even in the garden of a house at Brocton!*

RAF Seighford's bomb stores had a capacity of 800 tons, held in four dumps each of 200 tons. These were half-hidden in an isolated wooded area and covered by long camouflage netting strung through chicken wire mesh supported by metal poles or the trees themselves. *The bombs were brought by railway to Great Bridgeford then driven to the airfield.*

The intensive flying programme created a huge demand for fuel. Air Ministry policy decreed that an RAF station should have storage capacity for six weeks supply. The petrol was kept in underground tanks, each holding 12,000 gallons. The permitted maximum for one storage unit was 72,000 gallons so an airfield had to have several dispersed installations. Seighford had two units: one of 72,000 gallons near Hextall Covert and a smaller one of 48,000 gallons beside Bunns' Bank.

One of the training exercises carried out at OTUs was fighter affiliation in which fighter aircraft made mock attacks on the Wellingtons *to give the bomber crews, particularly pilots and air gunners, experience in engaging enemy planes at close range and instruction in combat manoeuvres.* No.1686 Bomber Defence Training Flight provided this service for the trainee crews of 30 OTU.

I remember the first Wellingtons being flown in, along with a number of Miles Masters for training the air gunners. The Masters' job was later taken over by Hurricanes.

I had to stay alert during the long hours of our cross-country exercises as we were liable to be intercepted somewhere along our course by one of 1686's Hurricanes. The fighter and I (as the Wellington's rear gunner) had 'camera guns' with 200 feet of film to record the outcome.

A 'Bullseye' was one of the final flights on the course. The crew was briefed as though it was a real operation, and flew a dog-leg route to a specified target. Sometimes this was the King George V Docks in London or a bridge site in Wales. The London flight could have Army personnel on board to assess the capital's defences and searchlights. The simulated raid also involved mock attacks by night fighters.

Some of the trainee crews flew air/sea rescue missions. The more experienced crews could also be called on to help with special flights to divert enemy defences from main bombing raids.

Some of our Wellingtons were roped in to fly in one of the 1000 Bomber Raids.

✻　　　　　✻　　　　　✻

I used to help with preparation for the later Thousand Bomber Raids. This meant using any aircraft that could fly. I would go on duty when the aircraft were lined up on the runway at Seighford. Five or six per night were used depending on how many aircrews were available as they had to be on their final two or three training flights at the OTU.

My duty was to ensure the Wellingtons were airworthy and ready to fly. I checked wings, ailerons, rudders, tyres etc. I would help haul the bomb trolleys under the aircraft but the actual bomb loading was the duty of the armourers. Then it was off duty until it was time for the aircraft to return.

The aircraft counted towards the 1,000 but flew on diversionary raids to easier targets in France, Belgium or even Germany to draw enemy defences from the main raid. It served as a training flight but counted as an operation. Everyone went to make up the crews, even a padre and a doctor.

✳   ✳   ✳

I was taken on a family outing on the country bus to Seighford to see the aircraft. We walked along a road that bisected the camp. We came to a servicing hangar where there was a Wellington that had holes the size of dustbins in its wings and fuselage. There was a Senior NCO standing there and Dad asked him if I could look over the aircraft. The Sergeant said I could but not Dad. I was taken into the Wellington and shown all the various positions. The impressions gained have remained with me all my life, in particular the strong smell of the aircraft.

In conversation he told Dad that the Wellington had returned two days ago from a 1,000 Bomber Raid on Germany and in the course of it had been badly knocked about.

The final task on the training course was a night flight over enemy territory, usually France. The object of this 'Nickel Raid' was to drop not bombs but propaganda leaflets. *These trips were supposed to be fairly safe and provide pre-operational experience. However anything could go wrong from the weather to a Jerry fighter – bad news for a sprog crew.*

✳   ✳   ✳

The trainee crews were sent out to allegedly soft targets – but one or two came back to Seighford badly shot up.

At least eight 30 OTU aircraft never returned from their Nickel raid. Of these, three were brought down over France (five crew were killed, seven survived to become prisoners of war and five evaded capture); one had to ditch in the Channel (the crew were injured but retrieved by an air-sea rescue launch – only to be killed over Germany with their new squadron a mere six weeks later); and four made it back to England only to crash before getting home (happily the crews of two of these aircraft were able to bale out without injury).

For those crews who got through their OTU training and their Nickel raid the future was a posting to a Heavy Conversion Unit where they acquired two new colleagues – a flight engineer and a mid-upper gunner – and the skill to fly the big four-engine bombers. Then it was on to the real thing with an operational Bomber Command squadron.

This is the story of just what lay ahead for one crew who came together at Seighford. Scotsman Thomas Forbes had joined London's Metropolitan Police in 1932 and was still serving in the city at the time of the Blitz. His reaction to the carnage was to fight back – by joining the RAF. After basic training, Tom Forbes was earmarked as a potential pilot and sent to 2 British Flight Training School in California.

Tom Forbes and his crew training at Seighford, 1943

Having qualified for his 'Wings', he returned to England for operational training. At 30 OTU he crewed up with navigator Leslie Matthews, bomb aimer Frankie Thomas, wireless operator Reginald Sneesby and air gunner George Deasley. Their course at Seighford ended successfully on 23 March 1943 with a Nickel flight to Lille.

After four weeks at 1656 Heavy Conversion Unit at Lindholme, they were posted to Wickenby to fly Lancasters with 12 Squadron. Their first operation followed on 23 May, and they were soon in the thick of it over Germany with a further seven raids.

The crew survived without harm until 25 June. That afternoon Reg Sneesby did a favour for another crew who were lacking their own wireless operator with a flight test pending. He stood in for the absentee and the flight was able to take place. The Lancaster disintegrated in mid-air and crashed with the loss of all seven on board. Reg was 21 years old.

The last mission of the Forbes crew was on 12/13 July 1943. They were returning from a successful raid on Turin but their Lancaster came down in the sea just off the coast of France. Only Leslie Matthews survived of the four men who had trained with Reg Sneesby at Seighford – Tom Forbes, Frankie Thomas and George Deasley were lost in the crash.

3

THE FIRST YEAR

Twenty-six Wellingtons and their groundcrews arrived at Hixon from RAF Finningley at the beginning of 1943. The two flights moved on to Seighford immediately to form the basis of the new station that had been officially opened on 1 January. The following selection of incidents gives an idea of the work, and the trials and tribulations, of 30 OTU at Seighford.

The first loss of an aircraft occurred on 7 February 1943. Sergeant Browning of the Royal New Zealand Air Force had already made two attempts to land. He came in too fast on the third approach, overshot the end of the runway and finally landed in a field. Luckily there were no injuries.

Wellington Z1683 was destroyed attempting to take off on 22 March. The starboard undercarriage collapsed and the aircraft caught fire as it skidded to a stop. Evidence at the following enquiry suggested that the pilot had unintentionally selected the 'undercarriage up' control while he was still on his take-off run.

DF641 had its own problems on the same day. It came in to land after a bombing exercise but overshot the runway and had to make a belly-landing. The pilot, Flight Sergeant Lewin, reported that instrument failure had prevented him putting the propellors into fine pitch for the landing. The cause of the failure was traced to a broken pipe line.

This Wellington was lost in a freak accident fourteen months later on a flight from Hixon. During the night of 27/28 May 1944 it was over Lincolnshire when the dinghy broke adrift and created such damage in the fuselage that control of the aircraft was lost. The plane broke up in the resulting dive and caught fire on impact. Seven aircrew died in the accident – the cause of which was put down to either the dinghy release mechanism being faulty or a member of the crew turning its handle in mistake for the heating control.

A double tragedy struck Seighford on 10 April 1943. The accidents were within fifteen minutes of each other although 30 miles apart. BK179 took off at 0510 on a bombing exercise. Five minutes later it appeared to stall before crashing in Ranton Woods, two miles from base, and catching fire. All five crew, Flying Officer R Haynes and Sergeants T E Jervis, L R Bray, R F Knight and F Yates, were killed in the crash which local people remember with horror:

I was woken up and saw a fire in the wood across the fields.

            ✳   *✳*   *✳*

The Wellington ploughed through the wood, cutting down many trees and leaving a trail of dead pigeons.

            ✳   *✳*   *✳*

The woods were burning well after the crash. One body was hanging from a tree.

Flying on the same bombing exercise, Wellington DF611 had taken off twenty minutes before BK179. One engine failed at 0530. When the other began to lose power, the pilot decided he had to attempt a forced-landing. They were over a Peak District hillside near Hartington but he spotted a stretch of the Buxton to Ashbourne road and attempted to land in a field alongside. The aircraft slithered across the field, smashed through a stone wall, crossed the road and ploughed through the opposite wall. The collision split open one of the wing fuel tanks and the Wellington was burnt out in the fire that followed. Flight Sergeant Ronald Jones the pilot, navigator Flight Sergeant John Spencer and bomb aimer Flight Sergeant Gilbert Parsons were killed in the inferno but wireless operator

*A Seighford Wellington, 1943
photograph by Walter Carter*

Flight Sergeant R J Perrin and rear gunner Flight Sergeant J Douglas escaped with injuries.

The backbone of Bomber Command's operations was the four-engine Avro Lancaster. One made a test landing at Seighford on 21 May 1943 to check the suitability of the runways for future use. The result was adequate and many 'Lancs' landed at the airfield during the next two years. Squadron Leader Leslie Goodman was Acting Station Commander one night in August 1943 when he was ordered *to prepare the station to receive twenty-five Lancasters which were on the famous Peenemunde mission. The planning and the execution taxed our resources, but in the event only a much smaller number arrived.*

The wear and tear on 30 OTU's Wellingtons by their constant use was illustrated on 22 May when DF546 swerved on take-off and the undercarriage collapsed. The cause of the accident, which wrote-off the plane, was traced to faulty brakes. Oiling up, faulty valves and a build up of pressure in the drum had the effect of the starboard brake being applied.

Human error was the cause next day when BK251 was damaged during take-off. The pilot, Sergeant Lydon, tried to stop when he realised that the air speed indicator was not working but he was too late to prevent the plane hitting the airfield boundary. The CO's verdict was 'carelessness' as the pitot head cover had not been removed during the pre-flight check.

BK142 took off from Seighford at 1215 on 19 June. There was an engine problem at 1240 and the plane crash-landed two miles short of the airfield. Two of the crew were injured but all got out before fire destroyed the Wellington.

Eight aircraft bound for Nickel raids took off from Seighford between 2255 and 2307 on 1 July. Five of them returned safely and the sixth landed at Hixon shortly afterwards. BK255, however, had been hit by flak and the pilot had to opt for an emergency landing at Exeter. The starboard engine was on fire as he began his attempt; then the port engine failed on the approach to the airfield. The Wellington crashed and burnt out. Four of the crew, Sergeants L W Fisher, M Bloomfield, K R Burrows and S E Pegg, died; only the rear gunner, Sergeant B S Sheldon, survived although injured. The eighth aircraft was also in the vicinity of Exeter and managed to get down safely by using the searchlights that had tried to guide in the luckless BK255.

Seven Seighford Wellingtons took off on Nickels just before midnight on 5 July. Sergeant Cook had engine trouble and called 'Darky' at RAF Church Broughton in Derbyshire. He was able to land safely at Ashbourne at 0128. Darky was the radio system for aircraft who were in trouble and seeking a homing signal to guide them in for an emergency landing at the nearest airfield.

Distinguished visitors arrived at the airfield on 22 July – General Eaker, American Officer Commanding European Theatre of War, and Controller Knox of ATS (Auxiliary Territorial Service) inspected a guard of honour of RAF and

WAAF. Ira C Eaker had come to Britain as the USAAF's observer in August 1941. He returned to the States and was heavily involved in the preparations to bring the Eighth Air Force to England.

Many American planes and personnel visited Seighford and Hixon during the War. The USAAF had a crew replacement centre at Yarnfield near Stone and they used the local RAF airfields on numerous occasions.

Seven aircraft left Seighford on a Bullseye mission on the night of 28/29 July. Sergeant Aspin in DF640 had to land at Harwell, Berkshire with an overheated engine.

Six aircraft took part in an air/sea rescue flight on 30 July. Four more flew a similar mission on the next day, and a further two on 2 August. There was no luck with any of these searches.

Its undercarriage collapsed when Wellington BT356 landed after a bombing exercise on 7 August. It was a perfectly acceptable landing; no blame was attached to the pilot, Sergeant Birchall, as the collapse had been caused by an internal crack in a bracing strut.

HE390 was engaged on routine circuits & landings on the morning of 11 August. At 0940 a Miles Master from 5 (Pilot) Advanced Flying Unit at Ternhill in Shropshire came out from the clouds at about 800 feet. By terrible misfortune it was too close to the circuiting Wellington and a mid-air collision was unavoidable. The wreckage fell on land belonging to Derrington Farm and Vicarage Farm near the airfield. All five men in the bomber (20-year-old pilot Sergeant Spencer George Cochrane, instructor Flight Lieutenant L W Metcalfe DFC, navigator Sergeant E W C Bryant, air bomber Sergeant C Yates and 33-year-old rear gunner Sergeant Frank Powis) and the two crew in the Master, Sergeants C Simons and J W Mudie, were killed.

I was about thirteen and on the school summer holidays. I was working with a pitchfork to help with the harvest at a farm near Derrington. There were planes over Seighford as usual. I spotted a little Miles Master as it dived at a Wellington. I thought it was giving it fighter experience. I assumed the Master pilot must have misjudged his approach as there was a loud bang as he flew into the bomber at a fair old rate. It ripped the wing off the Wellington and both planes fell in a ball of fire.

Wellington HE390 had been involved in a much less serious incident four months earlier when it ran into a Lysander while taxying. The Lysander was written off but the bomber only needed a few repairs. HE390's pilot at the time, Flight Lieutenant Spurr (Royal Canadian Air Force), completed his OTU course only to be killed on operations with his new squadron within weeks.

There was another casualty of that mid-air collision on 11 August. Flight Sergeant Mace (Royal Australian Air Force) was taxying along the runway in Wellington DF640 at the time but swung off on to the grass and hit a tractor. It was recommended that his logbook be endorsed for 'carelessness' although it was noted he may have been upset by witnessing the crash of the other two aircraft.

DF640 was to meet its own tragic end on 26 April 1944. It bounced badly on a landing at Hixon and had too little height when the pilot tried to go round again. Three of the crew died when the plane flew into Weston Bank.

Pilot Officer Brook had to make an emergency landing on one engine in HE481 on the afternoon of 20 August. To make matters worse, the airfield at Barkeston Heath, near Grantham, was out of service at the time and there were obstacles on the runway. Despite all the hazards, the crew survived with minor injuries.

Screened navigator Walter Carter was on board that flight as an instructor. *The pilot had feathered the starboard propellor for practice but was unable to unfeather it. We lost height steadily and picked out a likely-looking airfield. Unfortunately the runway was under repair or being lengthened. At any rate there was not enough length and we ran into a big heap of bulldozed earth, barbed wire and other rubbish. The front turret was stove in and the undercarriage collapsed. Fortunately the front gunner was out of the turret as we had all assumed crash positions. But I had forgotten to do up the pilot's harness and he was thrown forward on impact and gashed one hand.*

We were carrying 11.5lb. practice bombs and as we slid along on our belly these activated and the fuselage was filled with white smoke. We got out quickly through the astrodome and starboard escape hatch. A head count showed that one crew member was missing so two of us went back in. We found the rear gunner collapsed in the fuselage just forward of his turret, gasping for air. So we lifted him out and he soon revived.

It was later revealed that the batteries were incorrectly connected thus causing the lack of sufficient power to unfeather the propellor.

There was a spate of mechanical problems on the night of 23 August. Eight aircraft took off for Nickel raids. Two of them returned two and a half hours later with turret trouble, and a third landed at Middle Wallop in Hampshire for the same reason.

BK359 was destroyed after an unusual collision on 26 August. It was taking off but swung onto the grass (due to a gusty wind and the pilot spotting workmen in front of him) when about 350 yards along the runway. The aircraft was now approaching the men and the pilot, Pilot Officer Vernon, tried desperately to continue his take-off. Unfortunately the starboard wing hit the workmen's lorry and BK359 ended as a complete write-off in the centre of another runway. There was only one casualty, the lorry driver, who was taken to hospital with a leg injury. The pilot's log book was endorsed 'carelessness' despite the fact that the workmen had been repairing the runway while it was still in use.

After all the Nickel leaflet drops, Seighford aircraft were over enemy territory with real bombs on the night of 30/31 August. This was the first of a series of small raids in which OTU crews bombed ammunition dumps sited in forests in northern France. Each target was marked by Pathfinder squadron Halifaxes and Mosquitos with the purpose of accustoming the trainee crews to bombing onto markers.

Four of Seighford's Wellingtons were among the thirty-three aircraft which attacked the German ammunition dump in Foret d'Eperlocques near St Omer. BK146, X3565, HE507 and HE505 took off between 2024 and 2028. Three of them dropped their bombs successfully but the crew of X3565 failed to see the target indicators due to navigational difficulties. The pilot, Sergeant Gipson, returned to base after making safe his 4,000lb. bomb and jettisoning it on Cannock Chase at 0015. Two aircraft, from other OTUs, failed to return from this 'special task' mission which was regarded as successful as a large explosion was seen at the dump.

There was another enemy target the following night. Sergeant Gipson was airborne again with three other Seighford Wellingtons. Two of them successfully found the target in the Foret D'Heslin area but the other two had to return and jettison their bombs.

HE222 took off at 2125 on 1 September for a night navigation exercise. The crew reported a fire had broken out and one engine had failed. They decided to abandon ship when the second engine lost revs and power. The pilot, Flying Officer Whitehead, attempted to reach Seighford but the Wellington came down at 2230 to the north-west of Eccleshall. Two hundred personnel had volunteered to form a search party before the news was received that all the crew were safe.

It was back to France on 2 September with HE413 dropping seven 500lb. bombs on the Foret de Mormal but BJ358 returned early and had to dump a similar load in the sea off Rhyl.

It was an eventful night on 21/22 September when six aircraft left on a Bullseye but only one landed back at base. The others landed at Bircotes and Finningley.

On the night of 2 October 'D' Flight Navigation Leader Walter Carter flew with Flight Sergeant McInery's crew whose navigator, Flight Sergeant Trewavas, he regarded as the best pupil he ever supervised. The navigational log the trainee produced that night, considered to be a perfect example by his instructor, illustrates the hard work expected of the OTU crews. They were airborne at 1853 and set course for Newmarket. The route then lead to Newbury, Taunton, back to Newbury, then to Wallingford, Goole, Catterick and Newmarket, and finally home to Seighford. They landed back at 0059. *The six-hour trip plus the briefing and other preparations made such exercises a fairly long day or night's work.*

Sadly, like so many Bomber Command aircrew, 'Shorty' Trewavas did not survive the war.

Pilot Officer Ormerod attempted to land BK349 during circuits & bumps on 5 October only to have his undercarriage collapse. Fortunately there was no fire or injury, and the pilot was held to be blameless as the cause was due to metal fatigue – the undercarriage having suffered a succession of heavy landings.

A more serious accident occurred on 17 October. BK971 was taking off when the port engine failed. The pilot, Sergeant Williams, cut the throttles but was unable to stop before his aircraft crashed into some trees beyond the end of the runway.

Criticism for both the instructor and his pupil followed an incident on 24 November. The pilot was too late to correct a swing when X3813 was taking off. The aircraft was written off after colliding with a hut on the boundary of the airfield. The subsequent inquiry deemed the pilot had been guilty of an error of judgement but his tutor was also guilty of giving poor quality instruction.

Wellington X3883 left Seighford for a night exercise on 29 December. After a few minutes the starboard engine caught fire. When the pilot, Sergeant Collett, opened up the throttle, the port engine also burst into flames. He ordered the rest of the crew to bale out, and then jumped from the blazing plane. X3883 crashed at Hoar Cross near Abbots Bromley at 2140.

The pilot, though injured, survived but the other five crew had not left the aircraft and died in the wreck. They were Pilot Officer J W Lorrimore (air bomber) and Sergeants J Whitehead (navigator), H W Miller (wireless operator), and gunners Thomas Baden Joyce and Eric Alfred Dean. Thomas Joyce was 19 years old.

A Wellington aircraft based at Seighford landed in flames in our field; only the pilot survived. The plane blew up. The local fire engine arrived, and while attempting to pump water out of the pit gradually got pulled back until it got stuck. We had to pull it out with a tractor. While this was happening, the fire tender from the local aerodrome came and put the fire out with foam.

4

MEMORIES OF AN AIR GUNNER

Reg White is one of a rare breed of World War II veterans – a Bomber Command Rear Gunner. His memories of his time with 30 OTU make a fine overall picture of life at RAF Seighford.

After the pre-call up medicals, I reported to St John's Wood (Lord's Cricket Ground) in February 1943, had the usual service haircut, various jabs and was fed at the Zoo before going to Initial Training Wing at Bridlington, then to No.4 Air Gunnery School at Morpeth and, on passing out as a sergeant air gunner, arrived at Hixon in late July '43.

Here all the 'aircrew trades' were herded into a large room and told to sort ourselves out into crews. As a result, a few days later I found myself at Seighford with an Australian pilot, South African bomb aimer, English navigator, Australian wireless operator and myself as 'tail end Charlie', carrying out operational training in Wellingtons which had obviously seen better days.

We stayed at Seighford until the end of August, flying to various parts of the British Isles as we became more proficient. Firstly during daylight and then after dark (double summertime so the latter take-offs – even for circuits & bumps – never started before 2200 hours.

Every day there would be Wimpys in the air, usually two or three on circuits & bumps whilst another two or three would be further afield engaged on cross countries – bombing and gunnery exercises etc. etc., and of course the same activities would take place at night with the added excitement of Bullseyes and Nickel raids as the final honing took place.

There was the time we were being held in the circuit and became bored with going round in circles so we did a dogleg up to Stone to have a look at the Wrens (members of the Women's Royal Navy Service) on the boating lake.

And the time we came back from a cross-country with the port engine u/s. We rolled the full length of the main runway before coming to a standstill – quite interesting hanging out of the rear turret on a pitch black night and telling the pilot there were trees on both sides of us.

One night a Mosquito and myself spent an interesting couple of minutes over Lancashire shooting each other down with flashing lights – I swear I shot him down first.

Not every crew was involved in flying on a daily basis because there were other things to practice as well. Such as ditching drill (the poor air gunner had the job of getting the dinghy the right way up for the rest of the crew to climb in comfortably); baling out procedures (everything except the actual jump) which in the final analysis saved my life when it was jump or die; the decompression chamber to illustrate the need for oxygen above 10,000 feet (you start to act stupid without realising what you are doing if your supply is cut off); simulated raids with a 'speeded up' clock for navigators and w/ops whilst the rest of us could watch progress on maps outside the exercise area.

These ground activities were usually carried out at Hixon where the necessary ground facilities had been installed. The parachute and dinghy drills were carried out with the crew wearing their normal flying kit; in the case of the air gunner this meant full flying kit and parachute harness.

It was two crews to a hut with both being on the same part of the course so that disturbance within the hut was kept to a minimum in the interest of harmony; allowances being made for the odd late night in town.

We ate in one Nissen hut and used an adjacent one for recreational purposes – playing cards, reading, writing *letters or sitting around chatting when we were not off to Stafford. The weather was not too unpleasant at that time of year and we were able to stroll around in battle-dress when going to and from our billets, even in the early hours of the morning.*

Reg was present when RAF Seighford was visited by General Eakers on 22 July 1943 and found himself playing an unexpected part. *My logbook shows that we took off for a cross-country but returned after thirty-five minutes because of a 'duff' wireless. Whilst this was being repaired we returned to the locker room where we got lumbered for this guard of honour thing (someone thought it would be nice to have some aircrew on show). After a while everyone got fed up of just standing around so we stretched out on the grass (probably to recuperate from the previous night's visit to Stafford). Then, without warning, a miniature convoy swept onto the perimeter-track and headed very smartly in our direction – panic stations – we all scrambled to our feet and stood in some sort of a line as the general climbed out of his car and walked across in front of us on his way to the waiting Dakota. Now I might be wrong about this but I have visions of a half-smile on his face, but on the other hand it could easily have been a grimace.*

(Reg's mind can be set at rest by Sqn Ldr Leslie Goodman's report on the visit – *I was Acting Station CO when General Eaker, Commander USAAF in UK, landed at Seighford. I was ordered to provide and command a guard of honour. He seemed impressed.*)

Whilst this had been going on, our aircraft had been made serviceable and we duly took off to carry out the cross-country. This involved flying out over the Irish Sea, letting out a drogue on a wire to about 350 yards, and then while the pilot weaved all over the place I had to fire at the damn thing with live ammunition. Normally on completion the drogue had to be wound back in (by hand by the air gunner in full flying kit – not an easy task at 5 or 6,000 feet) and examined to see how many hits one had managed. But this time I was very lucky. One of my early shots had hit the shackle between the wire and the drogue and it went fluttering off into the blue, making the wire on its own very easy to wind in. All that was left to do was to explain to a suspicious armourer what had happened. Fortunately we had an instructor aboard who could confirm the details so I did not have to buy a new drogue out of my pay.

On 31 July my crew took part in an air/sea rescue over the North Sea, taking off at 1030 as the 'lead' aircraft (having an instructor on board as 2nd pilot or an extra pair of eyes). We got to our designated area and strung out into line abreast to carry out the 'box search' in radio silence. Due to low cloud and haze, visibility was only four to five miles and after a couple of legs, the other aircraft got lost. We did 'collect' another Wimpy which was going to formate on us until it found we had different markings and that my turret was pointed in his direction. The guns were ready to fire, just in case, because we had been warned that Jerry was flying captured aircraft in order to get close to have a go at us.

Apart from this we saw nothing but all our eyes were aching from looking at the sea (which was quite choppy) and searching the haze for other aircraft. We landed back at Seighford after a 5hr 35min trip, only to have a barney with the cooks who didn't want to feed us because we couldn't produce tickets.

At 2045 hrs on 24 August 1943 we took off in Wellington 'E' (a beast which had given us problems before) to carry out our cross-country No. 4. Extended flights away from base were on designated routes to various fixed points in the British Isles, with the crew carrying out tasks which simulated a trip over enemy territory and, for example, coming back with an infra red photo of a certain fixed beacon.

This particular route was over the Southern Counties and I think it was somewhere in the Salisbury area that the port engine gave up the ghost. Now this was not a very friendly thing to do because it meant we had no hydraulics for the flaps, landing gear or rear turret.

In the circumstances the skipper thought it would be a good idea to land as soon as possible (the thought of spending some time away from base never entered his head), so he called up 'Darky'. From the rear turret I could see some airfield lights not too far away – these promptly went out!!! – leaving us without a friend in the world.

After calling several times, the skipper (who was a very democratic Aussie) had a pow-wow with the rest of us. Although very hurt at the reaction from the airfield below, we decided not to do anything silly like dropping a practice bomb but to abort the cross-country and head for home base.

On entering the circuit, the skipper called up and informed control about our problem. We were then asked whether we were going to bale out or what. This involved another pow-wow and it was decided that we would stay with the skipper whilst he tried to land the damn thing (nothing to do with it being a dark night and us too frit to jump). So whilst the bomb aimer and navigator spent the next fifteen minutes pumping the landing gear down by hand with the emergency bottle we stooged around the circuit.

Eventually all was ready and we came in heading for the main runway from a long way out. I should mention that 'E' had a nasty habit of dropping the port wing at normal landing speed, even with two good engines, so it was a case of keeping up the speed as long as possible. As we came over the last two fields I could literally feel the skipper lifting her over the hedges so that as soon as we were over the runway he could cut the throttles and let us roll.

He succeeded very well for with just a little bump we were down, and then we rolled – and rolled and rolled – until we eventually came to a standstill. All I could see out of the rear turret was bushes on both sides of us. Rear gunners always play it safe on take off and landing by having the turret abeam so that they can get out or be got out!

When the skipper asked for the runway lighting to be reversed we realised we had come the full length of the runway. In fact when he swung the aircraft around to get back to the perimeter track the tail went off the end of the runway.

Our troubles still weren't over for, about half way back along the perimeter-track to dispersal, the starboard engine failed as well.

We were picked up by a crew bus and taken back to the locker room. Just as we got inside the door, the landline from the control tower came to life:

'F/Sgt McLachlan to report to the control tower immediately'.

Someone must have left the switch open so we then heard the following conversation:

'You wanted to see me, Sir.'

'See you, of course I bloody well want to see you! What sort of a landing do you call that? Don't you know the landing speed of your aircraft?'

There was a pause for about three seconds before the skipper replied (don't forget he was an Aussie with little respect for rank):

'Yes, I know the landing speed, but you don't know your bloody aircraft – and if you think you could have done better then I don't mind going back up with you so you can show me.'

'What do you mean by that?'

'Well, even with two good engines 'E' always drops the port wing at normal landing speed. So I decided it was safer to come in at a higher speed considering that it was the port engine that was duff.'

'Oh, I see, well ... '

Here the line went dead and we heard no more. The skipper was quite a bit upset and the rest of us weren't too pleased either. But when he got his logbook back at the end of the course there was an endorsement, in green ink, commending him for his actions in landing the aircraft.

Only a few days later we did our Nickel to St Malo. The raid, which actually counted as an operation, took place on 27 August 1943. We air tested BK358 – C-Charlie' – for twenty minutes at 1605 ready for the evening's entertainment. When I tried the guns I found that they had 'day tracer' in the belts so on landing I reported this and asked for 'night tracer' to be installed.

No one else in the crew had any problems so we took off at 1955 for St Malo. The trip down to the Southampton area (our exit and entry 'gate') being uneventful, we headed out into the Channel.

Once clear of the coast I tested the guns again and, to my disgust, found the tracer had not been changed. The day tracer was literally blinding me. However we decided to press on and hope for the best as we were only just going to 'nip in' over the French coast and back out again, leaving the paperwork behind us.

*All went well, and having delivered the papers, we headed back out to sea again only to find after a short while that a load of searchlights were waving about in front of us. It was decided that these must be on the Channel Islands and looking for us. So, a 'dog leg' to port for five minutes then a turn back on course – only to find the ****** searchlights still in front of us. The skipper decided that searchlights or not we would fly straight on and take a chance. Strangely the lights didn't seem to get much closer for quite some time and we realised that we must have been well past the Channel Islands by now. Then the penny dropped – the searchlights*

Souvenir of a successful Nickel raid
Reg White's memento of his flight to St Malo

were in England where a 'Bullseye' we hadn't been told about was taking place.

Needless to say, as we approached the coast every ruddy searchlight in the area tried to pick us out and we had to fire off the colours of the day a couple of times to get rid of them. Having convinced the Army that we were not part of *their exercise, it was a case of a quiet plod back to Seighford, debriefing and off to bed after a flight of 4 hours and 55 minutes.*

I still have one of the leaflets complete with crew signatures and oil stains from the bomb bay.

This ended our flying days at Seighford and within the next couple of days we were on our way to Hixon for onward posting to Heavy Conversion Unit. But, on arrival at Hixon, we were astounded to be met by the Service Police who took us into a hangar and insisted that we empty all our kitbags and spread the contents out so that they could be examined. (Aircrew usually had two kitbags; one for the normal service equipment and one for your flying kit including long-johns, thermal vests and thick socks.) Everything was checked very closely and then we were allowed to repack our gear. I can assure you that we were not very happy about this even when

Reunion at Poznan
Reg White visits the graves of his four crew members lost over Berlin on 27 January 1944

we were declared 'clean'. We found out that a service revolver was supposedly missing from Seighford and it was thought that aircrew might have spirited it away.

We moved on to 1656 Heavy Conversion Unit at Lindholme, and then on to 460 Squadron at Binbrook where we arrived on 23 December 1943.

We carried out six successful operations before getting 'the chop' over Berlin on 27 January 1944. Unfortunately everyone at the front end went down with the aircraft, leaving just the wireless operator, mid-upper gunner and myself as survivors. After making our first parachute jump, we spent the rest of the war as 'guests' of Adolf in various PoW camps.

The sad fact is that I am the only survivor of the five that made up the crew who flew at Seighford: one 'chickened out' at Conversion Unit, one got hospitalised with appendicitis and was replaced so we could progress to the squadron, and the other two including the pilot didn't manage to get out when we were shot down.

5

MORE LOSSES

1944 brought more operational incidents for 30 OTU at Seighford.

Wellington BJ897 suffered an engine failure on 21 January and had to belly-land on the airfield as the pilot could not maintain height on one engine. His failure to jettison petrol before the landing was criticised as it might have caused a more serious incident.

HE914 failed to return to Seighford from a Nickel raid on 28/29 January. The pilot, Sergeant Drinkwater (Royal Canadian Air Force), managed to get his aircraft back across the Channel on one engine but had to crash-land near Maidstone. Luckily there were no fatalities although he and one other crew member were injured.

Two Bullseyes were aborted on 16 February; one plane had instrument problems and the other was forced to return to base with a sick navigator.

There was sickness again four days later when seven Wellingtons were on an air-sea rescue mission. One of them returned early with a sick pilot, to be followed two hours later by a second whose navigator was ill. There was something of a jinx on this mission as another crew had to return with a damaged fin after a mid-air collision with an unknown aircraft.

Wintery conditions caused problems on 22 February when eight Bullseyes had to be recalled due to the weather.

There was another fatal crash at nearby Ranton on 24 February. HE903 took off at 1657 to join six other Wellingtons on a Bullseye flight. It contacted base at 2158 but nothing more was heard from the plane. Twenty-four minutes later it suddenly came down through the clouds in a steep dive and crashed into the ground. All six crew – pilot Flying Officer E Ryan, navigator Pilot Officer W O Thompson, wireless operator Sergeant D D Roblin, air bomber Pilot Officer Charles J Yates and gunners Sergeant D H Hearton and Sergeant W Corner – died in the accident. The cause was never found as the condition of the wreckage prevented the investigators making any decision on mechanical or technical defects.

Seighford's much used runways were in need of repair in March 1944. Their condition caused an accident on the 7th when HE732 was about to take off. The aircraft swung and the undercarriage collapsed after the starboard tyre burst. No blame was attached to the pilot, Sergeant Harvey (Royal Canadian Air Force), as the burst tyre was due to damage by a stone.

An order was issued immediately for the runways to be cleared of stones and repaired. However, one week later, three of the crew in BJ799 were injured when their port tyre burst on landing. Again the aircraft swung and the undercarriage collapsed. It was considered that the landing had been slightly heavy but not enough to burst a tyre. The rough surface of the runway was blamed – *repairs were still in hand*.

Six aircraft carried out an unsuccessful air/sea rescue mission on 25 March.

On the same day Sergeant Thompson (Royal Canadian Air Force) was in ME977 on a crew exercise and fighter affiliation flight. The Wellington bounced on landing and the pilot attempted to overshoot. He lost power when the throttles slipped back and he doubted if he had enough airspeed to clear the runway. The result was a landing with the undercarriage only partly down.

HE465 took off from Seighford at 0006 on 15 April for a night training exercise only to crash into a hill at Swansmoor near

Admaston a few minutes later. One crew member, Sergeant M C Pocock, survived the impact but was rushed to hospital with severe injuries and died a few hours later. The other four, Flight Lieutenant E J Bull, Flying Officers S J Pugh and R O'Neill, and Sergeant A Whitehead were killed outright. Sidney Pugh, the 24-year-old pilot, was still on Arsenal's books as a professional footballer.

BK347 was on a cross-country exercise on 21 April with a crew of seven. During its five and a half hour flight the Wellington strayed off course, probably due to an unserviceable compass. At 1615 it descended through the dense cloud, which had been present throughout the flight, to pinpoint its position. Tragically they were so far off track that the aircraft was actually over the North Yorkshire moors. It smashed into Whernside, 2300 feet above sea level, and six of the crew were killed. The rear gunner, Sergeant Marks, somehow

A 30 OTU line up at Hixon.
The nearest Wellington is the ill-fated BK347 which crashed on Whernside on 21 April 1944 (painting by Alan Preece based on an Imperial War Museum photograph)

escaped with minor injuries. Those killed were Flying Officer E M Barrett (pilot), Flight Lieutenant A Alderson (navigation instructor), Flying Officer R G C Brodie RCAF (air bomber), Sergeant P E Lomas (navigator), Sergeant N Skirrow (wireless operator) and Sergeant R C Holmwood (gunner).

Descending through cloud to pinpoint the aircraft's position when lost was a common cause of wartime accidents – the agonising decision to let down and hope that there were no obstructions, or else bale out and perhaps land in the sea.

A salvage team from 60 MU dug a deep pit on the hillside and buried much of the wreckage. Some pieces of the remaining debris could still be seen in recent years.

Sergeant Bowater successfully piloted LN533 back from a Nickel on 9 May only to have the undercarriage collapse on touching down. The cause was traced to a reconditioned tyre which had deflated after take-off. The station's operational records duly mentioned that *steps are to be taken to endeavour to supply only new tyres to OTUs.*

On the same night, Wellington ME977, back in operation after its crashlanding on 25 March, tried to land but overshot the runway and fell into a ditch.

The period of bad weather which delayed the D-Day landings on the Normandy beaches also affected Seighford – *I was a member of the Stafford branch of The Spotters Club who used to meet at John Bagnall's Garage. We had an afternoon trip to Seighford one Saturday, about D-Day time. It was filthy weather and pouring with rain as we arrived. A trainee pilot in a Wimpy was half way down the runway when he swung, turned a full 180 degrees onto the grass and one undercarriage collapsed. He ended his journey just in front of the control tower.*

Bad weather on 9 June resulted in a Halifax from the Royal Canadian Air Force's 425 Squadron having to land at Seighford on return from a raid.

Two days later one RAF aircrew member had a very brief but extremely sad time at Seighford. *I only visited the station for a few hours – I was sent there from Cranwell to have a decompression test for my suitability to pilot Mosquitos with the Photographic Reconnaissance Unit. I knew a pilot friend, Flight Lieutenant Alistair Maclean, had been posted to 30 OTU so I asked the Adjutant if he was still at the station. I was told that Alistair had been killed in a flying accident the previous day.* Flight Lieutenant Maclean had been the pilot of HE820 when it took off from Seighford for circuits & landings on 10 June. The aircraft appeared to make a normal approach but did not touch down. It attempted an overshoot at about fifty feet then banked and flew into the ground. The pilot and his bomb aimer, Sergeant D Kelly, were killed; the other three crew injured. The aircraft was destroyed by fire.

LN171 was damaged on 29 June when it swung while taxying along the perimeter-track. The pilot, Flight Sergeant Tobin

Flying Officer R.I. Varney's Crew at Seighford, 1944

(Royal Australian Air Force), tried to correct the swing by use of the rudder and opening the throttles to increase speed. When this manoeuvre failed, he applied full brake but the aircraft collided with a tree. Flight Sergeant Tobin was to have an eventful week – he had to make a single-engine landing on 5 July at Croft in North Yorkshire. Neither crew nor aircraft came to any harm.

There was another collision with a tree while taxying from dispersal on 10 July. This time the starboard wing of LN587 was the casualty. No disciplinary action followed as the cause was put down to errors of judgement by both the pilot and the marshalling airman while the dispersal was obstructed by a pile of sand dumped there by the Works Department without permission.

The question of further clearance of trees around the airfield had been raised some months before. The land officer for the area was told by his superior at the Air Ministry that Seighford was to be made fully operational and he was asked to arrange for the felling of trees in an extended clearance area. This was done quickly with the help of Venables of Stafford, the local timber company. A week later he was informed by his superior that the decision about the station's status had been changed again and the instructions were therefore cancelled. The land officer promptly explained that it was too late – the trees were already down.

A Wellington crashed just three and a half miles from RAF Seighford on 30 July but it was not one of its own aircraft. LP437, belonging to 27 OTU, had taken off from its base at Lichfield at 0210 for night bombing practice. At 0410 it stalled and crashed at Doxey Wood Farm on Thorneyfields Lane near Stafford. The plane caught fire on impact and the five crew, all Australians, were killed. Had it been making a vain attempt to reach Seighford? The flight path for its final moments would suggest that it had been.

There followed a grim spell for 30 OTU itself when it lost five aircraft in five days. Returning to its Seighford base after a forty-five minute flight on 7 August, JA533 suffered a fire in the port engine while it was making its final approach. The pilot, Warrant Officer A D Groome, managed to reach the runway and touch down. The flames were spreading rapidly along the wing so he braked hard and the crew got out even before the aircraft came to a halt. The Wellington was destroyed by the fire but the disaster could have been much worse – the plane had been on a gunnery exercise and there were nine aircrew on board.

Next day LN588 took off for fighter affiliation but suffered a hydraulics problem which meant a return to base with the prospect of a flapless high-speed landing. It duly overshot the runway and crashed.

During the night of 9/10 August HE828 had to be abandoned due to flak damage while on a Nickel raid. It limped back across the coast but the crew had to bale out near Dorchester. Then DF612 was written off in an emergency landing at Hixon on the afternoon of 11 August although all five crew escaped injury.

The costly episode was completed the next night when BK562 was lost during a cross-country exercise from Seighford. Some of the crew had managed to bale out before the crash in which three of them died. There had been an instrument failure while the plane was in cloud. It came down near the River Trent on the outskirts of Nottingham.

It was not only 30 OTU aircraft which came to grief at Seighford. The American Air Force's B-17 Flying Fortress 41-9019 was a casualty at the airfield on 5 September 1944. It was a long way from its home base at Deopham Green in Norfolk.

It could well have been the same incident witnessed by a Stafford schoolboy. *I was on my bike in the Butterhill area when I saw a B-17 at only a few hundred feet, firing distress flares. It managed to land on the main runway but came to a stop only just onto the peri-track towards the main buildings. The crash team vehicles rushed out. The rear gunner fell out like 'strawberry jam', the co-pilot looked dead, and the pilot was wounded in one arm. The badly shot-up plane had two engines out but he had landed it one-handed.*

With its long runway and usually benevolent weather, Seighford helped many aircraft from other units. The summer of 1944 for example saw that Halifax from 425 Squadron land due to poor weather on the night of 9 June; two Whitleys diverted from Ashbourne on 20 July; three Wellingtons from RAF Lichfield ten days later; one from 1511 BAT Flight with engine trouble on 3 August; and five Halifaxes from Blyton, Lincolnshire on 6 August. Later that month five Bullseyes from Hixon had to land at Seighford when their own runway was obstructed.

The list of wartime visitors goes on:

I saw Spitfires, Mustangs, Blenheims, a Barracuda, Marauders.

✻   ✻   ✻

One weekend a dozen Curtiss Commandos arrived from Barkston Heath – these, very few of which flew to Europe, were probably collecting men and materials when the USAAF depot at Stone closed down.

✻   ✻   ✻

I saw Ansons, quite a few Spitfires, the occasional Mosquito, the odd Beaufighter (a lethal-looking thing), a line-up of Mustangs, an Argos quite often, Mitchells; and the Wellington which was testing the secret new jet engine came over quite often.

✻   ✻   ✻

A squadron of Mitchells roared over Stafford at roof top height and landed at Seighford, possibly to refuel.

✻   ✻   ✻

One morning we went down from our hut to the airfield to find a couple of 'heavies' had dropped in overnight because their own base was fogbound. I think they were Halifaxes which, alas, all we trainees could do was admire from a distance. No chance of a close up inspection, and by lunchtime they had flown away.

In addition to its Wimpys, 30 OTU itself used a variety of other aircraft including Defiants, Lysanders, Martinets, Oxfords, Masters, Hurricanes and Tomahawks for support activities.

Wellington HE529 was a casualty on 18 September. Flight Lieutenant Kirkland (Royal Australian Air Force) was on circuits & bumps when the aircraft failed to get airborne and ran through the boundary. The port engine had failed. Neither the pilot nor the other five crew on board suffered any harm.

LN711 was written-off after just one circuit of the airfield on the night of 26 September. One engine failed as it took off. The aircraft overshot the runway during the emergency landing and was damaged beyond repair.

The 4th of October was a day of emergency landings at Seighford. BK556 had taken off from Hixon but was sent to Seighford when it developed hydraulic problems. The undercarriage was lowered by hand pump but the flaps were out of action when Flying Officer Clerici made a successful touchdown. Then Flight Sergent Green in LP616, also from Hixon, had to make a single-engine landing after his port engine failed.

Eight aircraft satisfactorily completed 'Sweepstake' flights on 14 October. Sweepstake was a diversionary flight to draw the enemy's attention from a main Bomber Command raid.

Events in Europe in September 1944 brought about a major change of role for RAF Seighford. On 28 October the station was transferred from Bomber Command to Flying Training

Command. Some of the 30 OTU crews had not completed their training when Seighford's involvement ended and had to finish their course at Hixon.

The end of 30 OTU's occupancy of RAF Seighford was marked by tragedy. The Fighter Affiliation Flight, now flying Hurricanes piloted by Australians 'resting' as instructors after a tour of operations, decided to pay a farewell visit on 25 October. Three of them flew over from Hixon and proceeded to treat the station, and the entire neighbourhood, to a tremendous display of low-level flying in V-formation. On the final pass they came lower than ever over the Control Tower and WT Section. The leader banked but his wingtip touched one of the trees near the WAAF quarters and the Hurricane smashed into the ground. The pilot, Flying Officer A V Browne (Royal Australian Air Force), had no chance of baling out and was killed instantly.

Many people, service personnel and civilians, remember the last flight of Hurricane LF170.

The three Hurricanes had landed at Seighford that morning and took off again about 45 minutes later. They flew out over Walton Hurst and made a very low-level pass along the runway and out towards Stafford Castle. Then they turned back across the airfield for a second pass. One Hurricane hit a tree, rose up into the air but fell back and crashed into the ground.

❊   ❊   ❊

The Hurricane was on a beat-up when its wing tip just clipped one of the trees past the water tower by the Officers Mess near the WAAF site. It went in by a little pool by the Mess. There was a row of trees. It was not trying to go between them but banked and the wingtip just caught the tree.

Sadly the final operational record for 30 OTU at RAF Seighford had to end with the words 'unauthorised and extremely dangerous low flying'.

6

TRAGEDY OVER CANNOCK CHASE

There was one incident during 30 OTU's time at Seighford which, grim though it was, could have been much worse.

A routine flight over the Cannock Chase bombing range turned to disaster on the night of 15/16 July 1944. Wellington NC678 was over the Sherbrook Valley when it was hit by flash bombs dropped from another aircraft and caught fire. The pilot, Sergeant D L Phillips (Royal Canadian Air Force), gave the order to bale out and held the plane straight and level so the other crew members could jump. Then he baled out and the Wellington crashed two miles north of Cannock. Unfortunately the other four crew members had not left the aircraft and were killed. The pilot was not to blame for their loss as the intercom had been damaged by the fire and they might not have heard the order to jump.

The crew who died were Sergeant J D D Watt (gunner) and three Canadians; Pilot Officer S D Mann (navigator), Flight Sergeant J H Jones (wireless operator) and Sergeant P C H Mullins (air bomber).

Although the official records give little detail, it is still possible to piece together the last few minutes of NC678 from eyewitnesses of the final stages of the flight of the stricken aircraft. Having taken off from Seighford at 2340, the Wellington was flying south over the bombing range when it was hit by the bombs from the other plane. Once the fire had taken hold, the pilot turned back in the hope of being able to return to base. The flames increased as they flew above Hednesford and Cannock. It was obvious they could not reach the airfield so the pilot held the Wellington steady while he thought the rest of the crew were baling out. Then, with the aircraft losing height but heading for the unpopulated expanse of Cannock Chase, he jumped.

The port engine was out of action and the plane went into a diving left turn. It had almost completed three-quarters of a circle when it skimmed above the A34 road at Huntington and smashed into a small spinney of trees on the Dog-in-the-tree Farm.

I lived in Chadsmoor at that time and stood with a young couple watching a bomber, on fire, travelling towards Stafford. I thought it was returning from a raid over Germany.

*   *   *

We were asleep when suddenly there was a terrific roaring sound and the room lit up as the bomber went over the top of the house on fire. It was a job to say how much it missed us by but it was very little. It was a ball of flame as it disappeared over the brow of the hill. The bomber crashed in a little copse. We went to see it but could not get close as there must have live ammunition on board and this kept exploding.

*   *   *

I had just come off duty at the small RAF camp at Pottall Pool crossroads. It was just after midnight and we were about to go to bed when the Wellington came very low over the row of houses where I was billeted. The fire beneath the fuselage lit up the bedroom.

It crashed into a large coppice of sycamore trees and the wings cut off trees about two feet in diameter. The engines buried into the ground and ammunition was exploding everywhere. Nothing could be done to save anyone.

*   *   *

I was sitting on the outside toilet at 26 Heath Street, Hednesford when I heard the roar of a plane with its engines spluttering. I went onto the yard and looked in horror at the plane with smoke pouring from it. Our next door neighbours had been woken by the noise and they too were horrified when they saw the stricken aircraft.

It was slowly coming down and made a tight left turn and I thought it might be heading for Seighford RAF station. It wasn't long after its left turn that we heard a muffled sound and we knew the plane had crashed not far away. I got on my pushbike and as I rode up Heath Street I could see huge clouds of black smoke in the direction of Pye Green. It was soon clear that it had come down at or near the Dog-in-the-tree Farm.

I was unable to get very close to the plane because of the intense heat. I estimate I was 200 yards away. As I stood there helpless, I felt what I thought was a stone under my foot. It was a small ballbearing which was still warm.

✻   ✻   ✻

The Cannock Chase range target –
but some bombs fell as far away as Brocton!

I was one of five lads walking along the A34 as we had missed the last bus from Stafford. It was about 12.45-1.00 a.m. when we saw a plane approaching. It lit up the sky. At first I thought it had released a flare then I saw that it was the aircraft itself which was on fire.

At that time the A34 was not dual-carriageway. The aircraft just cleared the hedge and crashed into the field about thirty yards from the road. A second earlier and it would have come down in the road.

One of the lads ran to the police station and the rest of us got into the field to try and help but the scene was horrific. The plane was a raging inferno and the bullets were going off. We searched the hedges and field as near as we could. We found an airman lying slightly embedded in the ground. He was not in flying kit, just a tunic with his shirt visible. There were no signs of any wounds or injuries but when an RAF ambulance arrived a nurse told us he was dead.

✻   ✻   ✻

The spinney was practically in the middle of what was then open fields. When the plane exploded on impact with the trees the wreckage was scattered for hundreds of yards. The field from the spinney to the farm lane was littered with debris.

✻   ✻   ✻

The Fire Service was soon on site. They left one of the Wellington's tyres burning so they could see.

✻   ✻   ✻

The plane had woken me up as it went over at rooftop height. The bedroom was as bright as day with the flames it was that close. A near neighbour and I arrived about fifteen minutes after the impact. We found one person 50-100 yards from the fire. He was alive then but died shortly after. He had CANADA on his shoulder flash.

I was told later that the pilot had baled out and was found with a broken leg by soldiers from the army camp at Pottal Pool crossroads.

Next morning I revisited the site. RAF men from Seighford were on guard duties. WAAF medics were getting the crew out. The last one was not found until later on in the day.

✻   ✻   ✻

My father-in-law was a member of the ARP. At the site next morning he found a wallet which he handed to the police. It belonged to a Canadian officer, and inside it was a photo of an Air Force officer and a lady, personal papers and a bent nail file.

✻   ✻   ✻

When daylight came we had a closer look. Close to a hedge we could see one of the crew. He had no parachute. His NAAFI card was sticking out of his tunic. He must have jumped out just before the crash. There was an imprint about six inches deep.

✻   ✻   ✻

The area was cordoned off and guarded by military personnel. After a period of time all the debris was removed except for small bits and pieces. The local people then searched the area for mementoes. In hindsight this was a bit morbid and gruesome but we didn't know at that time exactly what had happened.

There was a reminder of the crash in the 1950s when the farmland was being cleared for the building of the Dog-in-Tree housing estate – *parts of the plane, bullets and an airman's boots were uncovered.*

"It missed us by very little" – four men died when NC678 crashed that night in July 1944 but the toll would have been

much worse if the aircraft had come down a few seconds earlier and hit houses in Cannock.

30 OTU's losses over its three years of flying training reached a terrible total – 132 aircrew killed and 60 aircraft destroyed. In April 1944 alone the cost was 21 deaths, 4 Wellingtons destroyed and 2 seriously damaged.

Thousands and thousands of aircraft flights at Seighford and Hixon were normal and trouble-free but I was told that at one stage the Unit was losing one aircraft a week through crashes.

✻   ✻   ✻

After a cross-country, we had a prang at Seighford and I was taken to Stafford Infirmary with all sorts of complications. Then I was taken to the RAF hospital at Cosford and was there for Christmas 1943. While I was there, the rest of my old crew were killed.

✻   ✻   ✻

We would hear the planes circling – and could sense when something was wrong, such as coming in on one engine. We boys would race up on our bikes like mad. I've seen Wellingtons with bodies hanging out of them. Some came back dead in the planes and we saw them being carried off.

✻   ✻   ✻

It was in June '44. A Wellington on circuits & bumps came in to land but tipped onto its port wing. It slewed across the airfield in a shower of flames and debris, and ended in the stream. The crew were dragged out but they had burned to death, except for the rear gunner who survived with a broken ankle.

There were six or seven crashes that month and the C.O. told me this was the worst record in the country at the time. Senior officers came to investigate.

* * *

Many a plane came back skimming the trees on one engine.

* * *

One Wellington was flying low over the runway in its attempt to land. The rear gunner rotated his turret and jumped out before the plane actually landed.

* * *

I often stayed with my grandparents who lived in Long Lane, Derrington. I was outside one day when there was a loud bang. My grandfather came out and gave me a good telling-off for slamming the door. My denial was suddenly accepted when we saw black smoke billowing into the sky in the direction of the airfield.

Grandfather was the Special Constable for the neighbourhood and the fire engine stopped to collect him on its way to the site. Realising that the aircraft had crashed not far away, my mother and aunt took me there. The local policeman, 'Bobbie' Massey, ushered us away so we would not see the bodies of the crew when they were brought out of the wreckage.

* * *

I saw one Wellington in flames landing – it had lost all its fuselage fabric by the time it reached the end of the runway.

* * *

Despite the long runways several planes overshot. Quite a number finished across the Woodseaves road.

* * *

We often stood by a length of railings beside the main road to watch the aircraft. On one occasion a Wellington came thundering down the runway towards the main road but didn't manage to get airborne. It smashed through the fence and came to a halt right across the road. All traffic, including the local bus, had to be diverted along the bridleway behind the hangars.

Most take-offs however had a happier outcome. *A group of us were sat on the wooden fence on the Woodseaves road one morning. A Wimpy revved up and came roaring up the runway. The pilot could see us boys and he stayed low as he took off. We dived off the fence as the plane hurtled overhead. I looked up to see the rear gunner huddled over his guns – he grinned and gave a thumbs-up at the fright we had been given.*

7

AFTERMATH OF ARNHEM

The event in Europe that brought about the major change in role for RAF Seighford was the Battle of Arnhem. The famous airborne operation in September 1944 created a drastic shortage of glider pilots. An urgent training programme for replacements was drawn up and Seighford was soon heavily involved.

No.23 Heavy Glider Conversion Unit was formed on 28 October 1944 with the role of training pilots in readiness for the River Rhine crossings planned for March 1945. The Unit's main base was RAF Peplow in Shropshire but Seighford was designated as its satellite, hence the latter's transfer from Bomber Command to Flying Training Command. Twenty glider instructors reported for duty at Peplow on 29 October and the first use of Seighford followed on 1 November.

The towing aircraft for 23 HGCU's gliders was the twin-engine Armstrong Whitworth Albemarle. The gliders themselves, Airspeed Horsas and Waco Hadrians, were not sleek birds soaring gracefully on the thermals but massive troop-carrying heavy assault craft designed to be towed to within sight of their landing target before being released.

The Horsa was a fantastic glider with a very steep landing angle. They could drop it on a target the size of a dustbin. I managed to scrounge a flight in one. It was quite a thrill for as soon as the tow was dropped the pilot would stick the nose down, drop the flaps (which seemed as big as barn doors) and glide down like a hawk.

✻   ✻   ✻

The gliders were a sight as they dropped at steep angles and only levelled out at the last moment.

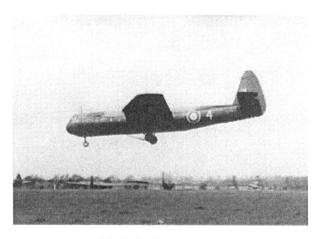

"It would glide down like a hawk" –
The Airspeed Horsa

There was some threat to local life and limb. The normal procedure was to drop the towing cable on the open expanse of grassed area on the airfield but ...

The tow cables were released at some speed and came snaking down at quite a rate.

Miscalculations caused damage in the neighbourhood – hence me helping to repair a barn roof at Brazenhill Farm.

*   *   *

I remember one incident when the tow cable must have snapped as half was dangling from the Albemarle and half from its glider. Even when under tow the cable sagged at quite an angle, especially if the glider was unladen.

Another potential problem with the relatively light gliders was the weather.

We had to turn the Wacos and Horsas into the wind and tie them down with round concrete 'cheeses'.

*   *   *

An airman often had to sleep inside a dispersed glider to anchor it.

The new Unit's first work at Seighford consisted of two flights in the Albemarles on 1 November. Glider flying commenced on 3 November with just one tug and one glider. All the groundcrew had to be instructed in hooking up the tow cables and signalling. Ten glider tows were completed next morning despite the runways having to be changed due to strong winds. Flying in the afternoon came to an early finish when two American Air Force B-17 Flying Fortresses landed and one of them got bogged down at the beginning of the runway in use.

The airfield was operational again next day and there was 'light flying' in the Albemarles without any tows. Things ground to a halt once more next morning when an Albemarle was marooned on the runway with a flat tyre. The other runway was still obstructed by the remaining B-17 so flying had to be abandoned. The problem was made worse by

The Albemarle served as the tow for Seighford's gliders

the fact that there was no spare wheel for an Albemarle at Seighford. Eventually one was brought from Peplow and fitted. It was 1700 before the job was done and the aircraft could clear the runway. The Flying Fortress was finally freed half an hour later and it took off for its home base.

Night flying with the gliders commenced on 7 November but the weather made itself felt again on the 9th when flying was delayed due to *icing conditions, the first of the winter.*

There was an incident on 13 November when Flying Officer Cave and Flight Lieutenant Moorhouse were piloting Horsa RX647. The tug aircraft started to descend just as their glider went up to the 'high tow' position. They were then at too steep an angle on the tow and had to make an early release of the cable. They made a successful forced landing at Ellenhall Park.

It was on 16 November when a well-remembered American invasion of Seighford began.

It was one of the bad days of what was to be a very bad winter. I was sitting at my school desk in Stafford when we heard the sound of aircraft. Then Fortress after Fortress appeared out of the fog and disappeared back into it just as quickly.

A total of 30 B-17s landed at Seighford that November day. They had been returning from a tactical bombing operation in support of an American infantry attack near Aachen but their East Anglia bases had become covered with fog before they could land.

The whole country was fogbound and Seighford was about their only chance. Conditions got so bad they were very lucky to get in even there.

*   *   *

There was great local excitement when the Fortresses arrived. I think one crashed on landing.

*   *   *

A Yankee big-wig arrived in an Argos to sort things out when the weather improved a little. The stranded aircrew were accommodated at the USAAF Depot at Stone.

The local fog cleared by the following afternoon. Flying was about to commence at 1445 but a further twenty-five B-17s were diverted to Seighford. The planned night flying for the gliders had to be cancelled due to the saturation of available space. *The fifty-five bombers were parked all over the grass on the north-east of the drome.* It was the 18th before the visitors could return to their own bases. Some got away around midday and the rest took off from 1500 onwards.

Even experienced instructors could make mistakes. The trainee pilot of Horsa RX639 made a heavy landing on 20 November. When the glider bounced, the instructor for some reason pushed the stick forward and damaged the nosewheel.

There was a more serious accident next day. Glider RX660 was written off when it made an unsuccessful landing in a field near Gnosall. At the moment he was releasing his tow, the pilot of the tug had to take violent action to avoid another aircraft. The manoeuvre put the glider in an awkward position and its pilot had to attempt a forced landing. The Horsa was wrecked when it hit a tree and went through a hedge.

Massed landings were practiced on 22/23 November when the gliders took off from Peplow and came down at Seighford. *Actual troop-carrying exercises took place occasionally – paratroops in their round crash helmets could be seen running round the woods.*

There was another accident on the 24th but this time it was one of the tug aircraft that was lost. The Albemarle was towing at 600 feet when its port engine failed. The glider cast off without any problem but the tug would not maintain height on one engine. The pilot, Flying Officer Marsh, could not feather the port engine as he needed both hands to control the aircraft. He realised he could not clear an approaching hill so he attempted a belly-landing. Marsh did all he could to save his Albemarle but it was wrecked when it came down near the top of the hill. The cause of the engine failure was traced to a piston – part of it and its ring were found in the oil filter.

The wear and tear of the training programme was illustrated by an unusual accident on 3 December. A Hadrian was over Hyde Lea near Stafford when the fabric on the fuselage's underside tore across its whole width and nine feet in length near the tail. The pilot was unable to contact his tug pilot by radio telephone so he tried to fly out to the side to attract attention. This also failed, the size of the hole was getting worse and the wind was making the tail balloon out. So the glider pilot opted for a forced landing before the fuselage suffered any more damage. He got down successfully in the Thorneyfields Lane area, avoiding both casualties and the loss of his Hadrian.

The glider came straight through the hedge in the dip over the brow of the hill from Newport Road, crossed the road and through the opposite hedge into the next field.

The reason for the accident was an accumulation of wear. The groundcrew had failed to discover the deterioration as the fabric looked in order. The implications were taken so seriously that the ACC in C/Group demanded a report on the eradication of the problem.

Mass landings ended with a multiple ground collision on 4 December. Horsas RX608 and RX625 landed safely and finished their run near the end of the main runway. Then RX678 landed only 150-200 yards short of them. The pilot failed to lower his flaps and ran into the other two aircraft. The Wing Commander duly recommended that he be removed from First Pilot duties.

Flying in cloud caused trouble on 6 December when the pilot of Hadrian 243666 experienced severe bumps and was forced to release from his tug. The glider broke through the clouds at 400 feet above the airfield, landed on the runway but then overshot and ended thirty yards into a ploughed field. The undercarriage was damaged when the Hadrian skidded sideways. The pilot was criticised for the line of his final approach but the pilot of his tug was also criticised for not avoiding the clouds in the first place.

Albemarle V1975 had problems on 17 December. The aircraft began to vibrate violently as soon as it touched down. This continued right through the landing. Various pieces of equipment were thrown into the cockpit; instruments and components were damaged. The problem had been caused by part of the airframe breaking due to previous heavy landings.

Memories of the B-17 invasion back in November were aroused on the 18th when a Liberator bomber dropped out of a passing formation of twelve and landed short of fuel.

There was another landing collision between Horsa gliders on 21 December. RX682 ran into RX700 which had landed just ahead of it. The pilots were not blamed as it was felt the flying control officer was at fault for ordering their simultaneous release.

As happened in 1943, the end of the year was marred by a fatal accident. About five minutes after it took off on 30 December, Albemarle V3944 suffered failure of its port engine at 250 feet. The aircraft hit the ground at Wincote, a mile south of Eccleshall, and burst into flames. All three crew, pilot Flying Officer Johnson, wireless operator Sergeant Terzza and Flying Officer Flack, were killed.

There were two pits in the field with a bank between them. The Albemarle slid across the first pit, hit the bank and stopped. As the plane lodged across the bank, both engines were catapulted out of the wings and fell through the ice on the second pit.

The farmer arrived and could hear the crew shouting and screaming but he couldn't get to them. The fire destroyed all but about two feet of one wing.

The tug had been towing Horsa RX629. This had to make a forced landing in the same field and was slightly damaged but the crew were unhurt. *I saw the tow plane and glider which landed in the field near Wootton. The glider later had its wings dismantled and it was taken back to Seighford airfield.*

The Unit's final incident at Seighford took place on 7 January 1945 when a Horsa was on night flying training. The pilot, on his first night solo, undershot the airfield due to casting off from his tug too early. His glider hit a fence near the beginning of the runway.

There was a cruel reminder next day that 30 OTU was still operating at Hixon. Wellington LN166 had taken off at 1035 on a high-level bombing exercise. All six crew were killed when the aircraft broke up in flight at 1130 and crashed beside the Stafford-Eccleshall road, near Pyebirch Manor, just two miles from Seighford airfield. Had they been heading there to make an emergency landing?

The aircraft, sounding in trouble, flew over Eccleshall before crashing at Pyebirch just over the hedge from the road. The road was closed while the recovery team from Seighford cleared the site of the main wreckage. This was piled up beside the road until collected. There was a big crater which was filled in later. Some of the fabric from the Wellington remained in the nearby trees for some weeks afterwards. The farmer found a glove with a hand still inside it when ploughing the field two months later.

* * *

A Wellington on fire came over Eccleshall from the Slindon direction. It hit the top of a Scots pine tree and crashed at the back of Willis's house (on the right of the road from Stafford).

There was a big crater which was filled in later. Wreckage was piled up beside the road. The top of the tree was badly bent over and this was visible for many years.

❋   ❋   ❋

I heard the stricken Wellington and saw it come down in a screaming dive. I knew it must have crashed nearby so I jumped on my bike to try and help. I was one of the first on the scene and was shocked by the horror I found there.

It was a black day for 30 OTU. Wellington HE853 had also taken off from Hixon that morning. Engaged on a navigation exercise beyond the coast, it acknowledged a wireless message from Bristol then nothing further was ever heard of the aircraft.

8

'THE SKY WAS FULL OF OXFORDS'

The news of the second and final change of use for Seighford was received on 11 January 1945. It was an indirect result of the terrible disaster at RAF Fauld in east Staffordshire on 27 November 1944. After the underground explosion of 3,500 tons of bombs, which claimed seventy lives, 21 Maintenance Unit had to move from Fauld to RAF Tatenhill. The knock-on effect was 21 (Pilot) Advanced Flying Unit, based at Wheaton Aston, having to relinquish Tatenhill as its satellite station. This role was then allotted to RAF Seighford.

No.21 (P)AFU's role was the further instruction of pilots who had undergone their basic flying training in the USA, Canada, South Africa or Rhodesia. These countries of vast cloudless blue skies hardly prepared the trainees for the weather conditions they would face over the British Isles and Europe. It was the task of the (P)AFUs to make up for this deficiency. Part of the training involved the use of the Beam Approach system for the pilot to align with the runway in bad visibility. Once the pilots were familiar with British flying conditions they could move on to the OTU stage of their training.

The Unit flew Airspeed Oxfords. The twin-engine 'Ox-Box', with its crew of three, was one of the RAF's standard trainers and almost every bomber pilot received instruction in one at some stage.

There was a delay in the (P)AFU taking up occupation of Seighford as 21 Group was informed on 18 January that the runways were in need of repair and the airfield would be unserviceable for some time. It was 28 February before the Unit was ordered to move in. The Commanding Officer at this time was Wing Commander Hordern AFC, *a very burly man who had played rugby for England in the 1920s.*

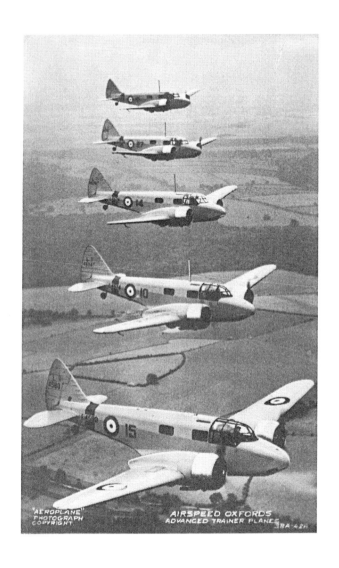

"The sky was full of Oxfords"
21 (P)AFU flew them in great numbers
(copyright Aeroplane magazine
www.aeroplanemonthly.com)

No.21 (P)AFU's occupancy was soon noted. *The sky was full of Oxfords – there were about a hundred on charge.* At least twenty of them were parked beside the now unused machine gun and cannon range in the south-west corner of the airfield.

The first recorded casualty happened within a week of flying commencing. On 7 March Oxford P9023 was written-off when the pilot made a bellylanding just after take-off. There was no evidence of engine failure and the trainee's logbook received a 'carelessness' endorsement.

NM631 was destroyed on 6 April. The aircraft overshot the runway then stalled. A wing dropped and hit the ground. The Oxford then landed heavily and bounced, tearing off the undercarriage. Although rain on the cockpit window had obstructed his vision, the pilot was considered to have made an error of judgement.

Everyone involved seemed to get some of the blame for a taxying collision between two of the aircraft on 24 April. P1923 had landed without trouble but then swung violently and hit the tail of LW865 which was still very close to the runway. The latter's pilot was blamed for causing an obstruction near the runway, Flying Control was blamed for not taking action to ensure the runway was clear for the second aircraft to land, and P1923's pilot was blamed for not overshooting when he saw the other aircraft too close in front of him.

The events of 27 April were far more serious when instructor Flying Officer Brown and second pilot Flying Officer Knight were on a night cross-country flight in LX486. Weather conditions were bad with snow and rain reducing visibility considerably. The pilot tried to lose altitude safely but flew into ground 650 feet high on Cannock Chase. Both crew were killed and the Oxford was destroyed by fire.

By now the war in Europe was drawing towards its end.

I was posted to Seighford from RAF Peplow at the end of February – it appeared to be a rambling dispersed station with not very much activity. Life was fairly quiet.

But some were still paying the toll. *Quite a few airmen came to The Staffordshire Advertiser's printing works towards the end of the War to pick up their former trade for employment when they were demobbed. They usually spent two half-days on their re-training. One aircrew member left us one afternoon to fly that night but didn't return next day. He had been killed when his plane crashed on the Wrekin in Shropshire.*

One immediate reward of the Allies' advance through Nazi-occupied territory in 1945 was the liberation of prisoner-of-war camps. A conference was held at Flying Training Command HQ on 2 April to discuss the repatriation of the PoWs. It was decided that Seighford would be one of the 'arrival station' airfields for the former prisoners returning

*Homeward bound
liberated PoWs head for an Operation Exodus Lancaster*

home. They were to be received and passed to their various personnel reception centres as quickly as possible. Hixon, which had been transferred from 93 Bomber Group to 21 Group Flying Training Command on 7 February, was to act as Seighford's relief airfield for this operation.

Transport Command's Dakotas were still heavily engaged in delivering war supplies so much of the burden of providing transport for the repatriation, codenamed 'Operation Exodus', fell on Bomber Command. With a few basic adaptations, a Lancaster was able to carry twenty-five passengers for the flight home from Germany. During a period of twenty-four days Lancasters alone flew 2,900 trips and ferried back 74,000 ex-PoWs to the reception camps.

Seighford's first contingent, twenty-eight men in one aircraft, landed on 18 April. Once they had disembarked from their aircraft, they received a medical inspection in a Nissen hut which had been specially erected near the control tower. There were powder sprayers for disinfection – the personnel employed on disinfection duties wore protective clothing consisting of combination suits, masks, goggles and hoods. *Some of the Exodus aircrew were dressed in white overalls and face masks to combat the threat of catching a contagious illness from their passengers.* The official records reported that the medical staff thought there was no evidence of gross malnutrition, considering how long the men had spent as prisoners.

Our ex-PoWs started arriving from all over the place. One weekend we had 72 kites – Lancs, Dakotas, Stirlings, Yorks and Americans. About 3,000 returning prisoners passed through Seighford.

*   *   *

One of the hangars was done up as a hotel and hostel. It was lined with flags and had hundreds of armchairs and settees.

There was NAAFI equipment and a stage for the band to play on. It was a sight to see when they came in. They crossed from the planes and the medical centre by bus to the hangars. They stayed one or two days before dispersing.

On 6 May a Mosquito landed at Seighford with a special ex-PoW. With a record of twenty-nine enemy aircraft destroyed, one probable and another six damaged, Wing Commander 'Bob' Braham had become WWII's most highly decorated fighter pilot in the RAF and Commonwealth Air Forces. He had been shot down over Denmark on 25 June 1944 and sent to Stalag Luft III. His captivity ended when the British 2nd Army liberated him on 2 May.

The most memorable day for people in the neighbourhood was 10 May. Air Vice Marshal Champion de Crespigny, ACC of 21 Group, attended for the arrival of a large Exodus contingent – forty-one Lancasters landed 922 ex-prisoners between 1645 and 2050. The men were from all the services and of many nationalities, including officers and other ranks from the RAF and various Allied Air Forces, Indian soldiers, and even seamen from the Chinese Merchant Navy. At one stage during that day there was a magnificent array of thirty-three Lancasters lining Seighford's perimeter-track.

The fleet of planes were coming down nose to tail – so close together that the duty pilot was blasting off red flares to try and slow things down (unsuccessfully).

The work continued until an order for the disbanding of the organisation was received on 29 May. Possibly the happiest man involved in Operation Exodus at Seighford was Donald Mould – *a Stafford lad, he had joined the Army early in the War and been posted abroad. After four years as a PoW, his prison camp was liberated and he was taken to an aircraft with the news that they were being flown home to England. His plane duly landed and he jumped down onto the tarmac, the first English ground he had touched for a long time.*

Not knowing he was at Seighford, he looked round at the surrounding countryside. To his amazement there, across the fields, he saw the familiar sight of the towers of Stafford Castle – he truly was home.

The eighth of May brought the news everyone who served at Seighford had been working for – Prime Minister Winston Churchill announced that Germany had surrendered.

Everybody from the villages congregated at the airfield. There were bonfires, rockets and the band playing.

✳   ✳   ✳

The RAF lads were chucking hand grenades in our farm pond and making great splashes.

✳   ✳   ✳

I spent VE Day with a curvaceous WAAF from 16MU at Stafford. It was a lovely night.

Within a day or two, however, it was a case of return to normal duties. The flying training continued; and so did the toll. The pilot of Oxford N4597 was killed while engaged in solo training on 13 July. During 'unauthorised low flying' near Little Eaton in Derbyshire, his plane hit a tree at high speed and disintegrated. The Court of Inquiry considered it to have been a flagrant disobedience of orders and misjudgement of height. It was felt that full publicity should be given to this accident throughout the RAF.

A less serious incident had occurred on 4 July when Oxford LX239 was taxying to its dispersal at 0130. The aircraft collided with another Oxford, ED134, which was stationary and unoccupied. There was no blame to the pilot however as he had moved forward in response to the directions of the marshaller's torches. These directions turned out to have been careless movements by the marshaller and not signals for the pilot! Disciplinary action followed for the errant torch waver.

More victory celebrations followed when Mr Atlee announced Japan's acceptance of surrender terms on 18 August 1945. There was very little flying activity – by now the main question in most minds was 'When do I get demobbed?'.

VJ Day was duly celebrated at Seighford. A visiting Flying Fortress took a party of ATC cadets on camp from Birmingham for a local flight.

Both the RAF and USAAF continued to use Seighford extensively until mid-1946. No. 21 (P)AFU was still involved in its role of pilot training and although the hostilities may have ended, the risks facing the trainees had not – peace did not bring an end to the fatalities.

Just after 1400 on the afternoon of 28 August Flying Officer Stratford, with Flight Sergeant Evison as his wireless operator, took off in Oxford NM640. Fourteen minutes later, three Dakotas were observed flying in formation 1,000 feet above Seighford's left-hand circuit. The Oxford was seen converging on them at about the same height. It went into a steep right-hand turn, paused for a second and then went over onto its back. The aircraft began to spin and hit the ground near Waltons Rough. Flying Control were alerted immediately by the pilot of one of the Dakotas and help rushed to the crash site. Nothing could be done – the Oxford had disintegrated completely on impact and both crew were killed instantly.

It was thought the pilot had suddenly seen the three Dakotas and took avoiding action by pulling the nose up and turning violently to the right. The aircraft had stalled in this steep bank and there was insufficient height to recover from the resulting spin.

There was a ground collision on 4 September. While taxying for take-off in BG646, the pilot failed to notice his aircraft's low brake pressure. He was unable to avoid hitting LW739 which was stationary while waiting for its own take-off.

The next major incident involved Oxford HN594. Navigation instructor Warrant Officer Robinson took off from Seighford on 28 December for an afternoon flight with Flying Officers Dowthwaite and Croker. They were typical 21 (P)AFU pupils who had learned to fly in South Africa and now faced British conditions. And typical winter weather it was – low cloud and showers.

It was to be a 140-mile flight, the first leg of which took them east into Derbyshire's Peak District. Robbie Robinson was at the controls as they reached the hills. Realising they were too low for safety he tried to gain another 200 feet of altitude but the Oxford could not respond. The aircraft hit the summit of Brown Knoll near Edale at about 100 mph.

Fortunately the angle of impact was not too severe. The Oxford crunched along for 150 feet before coming to a stop. When he regained consciousness, Flying Officer Croker found that he had been thrown out of the plane which was now little more than a wrecked heap. Somehow he had suffered little more than badly sprained ankles. He limped back to the shattered fuselage and found Robinson and Dowthwaite still lying in the remains of the cockpit. His fellow trainee had a badly broken leg, and his instructor had a broken jaw plus serious leg and internal injuries. They were in trouble; daylight was fading and an air search would not be possible before the next morning. This meant a winter's night on the bleak hillside. Croker knew he had to find a house and raise the alarm. The rough terrain aggravated the pain from his ankles and he had to resort to crawling through the snow on his hands and knees. Eventually he got down into a valley and spotted a couple of houses. He was just able to give details of the crash and his colleagues's plight before passing out from pain and fatigue – he had dragged himself a mile and a half in atrocious conditions.

The ordeal for the other two crew members of HN594 was far from over. The mountain rescue team searched Brown Knoll for hours without success. Realising the dangers of continuing, they called off the search for the night at 2200.

Aircraft were able to help next morning and the remains of the Oxford were spotted at 1030. Assistance finally reached the two injured men after they had spent twenty hours on the hillside. Both survived their grim experience although Warrant Officer Robinson had to have his leg amputated.

There is an ironic twist to the story. George Robinson and John Dowthwaite had strapped themselves into their seats before the crash but suffered serious leg injuries; Flying Officer Croker had not been strapped in but was able to limp away with sprained ankles. A more severe injury might well have prevented him from achieving the successful career that lay ahead. After playing as a professional footballer with Charlton Athletic, Ted Croker became nationally famous as Secretary of the Football Association, and the radio 'voice' of countless FA Cup draws.

An error by a member of the ground crew nearly caused a serious accident at Seighford on 21 March 1946. Oxford V3472 was engaged in circuits & bumps when the port elevator dropped off. The pilot managed to land successfully due to his skilful use of flaps and engines. The ensuing enquiry found that the groundcrew had not checked that the elevator securing bolts were fitted correctly. The flight sergeant was reduced in rank to corporal, and the airman directly responsible was court martialled.

Human error contributed to the loss of an aircraft on 24 April. Oxford LX134 took off for a night training flight but the starboard engine cut out when it was no higher than 100 feet. The pilot could not maintain height on one engine so he selected wheels up and belly landed. The plane came down near Hextall Farm and was written off although instructor Flight Lieutenant Booth and second pilot Sergeant Williams were uninjured. The reason for the crash was quite simple – the servicing nco had failed to refuel the Oxford before its flight. The pilot then compounded the error by failing to check the fuel level before take-off. He received a severe reprimand from the AOC.

There was just one more incident destined for Seighford's operational records. Flight Sergeant Tompson was on solo forced landing practice on 26 November 1946 when his port engine failed at 250 feet. So Oxford T1246 had to make a real forced landing with its undercarriage up in a field half a mile from the airfield.

So ended the recorded events of 21 (P)AFU at Seighford. Its training programme had reduced drastically once the war was over and its total establishment, which had once reached 148 Oxfords, had halved to 71 by Autumn 1946. On 5 December 1946 the Unit left its main base at Wheaton Aston and moved to Moreton-in-Marsh. The days of the Royal Air Force flying at Seighford had ended.

9

LIFE ON THE FARM

Clanford Hall is a eye-catching half-timbered building worthy of its 17th-century origins. RAF Seighford's airfield was literally on its doorstep – so close that it is extremely fortunate that the house did not have to be demolished like the Grange farmhouse. A few degrees one direction or the other and the lovely old property would have had to go.

The cluster of dispersal hard-standings and maintenance huts of 'D' Flight were very close to the farm buildings. At the time the airfield became operational Clanford was farmed by the Parrott family. For daughter Daisy it was a time when *we had a Wellington parked in our rick yard.* The harsh

Clanford Hall survived the construction of the airfield –
and the aircraft using the nearby runways

realities of war came home to this schoolgirl when she saw *there was a hosepipe at 'D' Flight to sluice out the remains of dead aircrew.*

A good many of the airmen spent a lot of time at the farm. My father had served in the First World War and he made them very welcome.

Vic, our farm dog, was almost a mascot for the aircrew. He used to go up on the long flights three days a week – the RAF saw more of him than we did. He also used to chase the aircraft along the runway. Many a time I had to collect him from the main Guard Room. One day he chased the wrong plane. It had some 'big-wig' on board and there was trouble. After that Vic was sent to our other farm near Stone.

The Parrotts left Clanford Hall in 1943 and the Browns arrived. Schoolboy Bill duly acquired a wealth of memories of his RAF neighbours.

The farm was smaller then and harvesting was done by hand in the war years. I got to know the blokes quite well when they came to the farm for eggs. They helped with the harvest for a shilling a night. My father would kill a pig, and my mother used to have a harvest supper. I remember seeing fourteen airmen round the kitchen table tucking into egg and bacon at eleven o'clock at night.

'D' Flight was based in the area now occupied by our 'new' cowshed. I used to play in the Nissen hut (a battery-charging shed and latrine) and the small arms ammo hut.

The groundcrew personnel used to wash their uniforms with aviation fuel then hang them in the adjacent wood to dry out.

When we were digging out the foundation for the new farm building we found dozens of bullets. In training belts, every so many bullets were made of wood to jam the belt and make the gunners practice release drill. These were painted red and the old hands would go along the rack as far as they could and pull out the clip, including two or three live rounds.

I got one flight sergeant into trouble. He let me play in the rear turret of a Wellington while he was doing something to the ammunition run. The guns were empty and I played with the twist handlebars, pretending to shoot down Messerschmitts. I was ordered out while the guns were loaded. The sergeant then signed the plane as serviceable for the crew to take over. But they found it wouldn't start – the batteries had been flattened by me rotating the turret while the engines were off. The aircrew spotted me and guessed the reason.

There were locked gates at either side of the runway where the road crossed. I even had to show my pass to go to school. The duty pilot with the Aldis lamp in the flying control caravan would show a green light when I could cross. New crew usually demanded to see my pass until they got to know me. The pass, a piece of paper issued yearly, was needed right through the War.

I got to know one Canadian pilot who, when on duty in the flying control caravan, would let me press the green light on the Aldis lamp. He used to come to tea at the farm. He was killed, soon after he left Seighford, flying Typhoons.

There were a great many American planes coming in to Seighford due to their base at Stone – Liberators, Mitchells, Marauders, Fortresses, Norsemen, and even a Catalina (a fantastic sight). A single B-17 once parked behind the farm on the 'D' Flight dispersal.

One foggy morning, visibility was 200-300 yards. I was leading our horse and cart along the wood on the runway side of Clanford Covert when I saw RAF blokes lining both sides of the runway and firing Very pistols. A Liberator was trying to get in and they were forming an approach path.

It landed long. The pilot saw the peri-track and swung towards it but missed. He managed to turn the plane in a great arc, missing the wood by fifty or sixty yards. The Liberator suddenly loomed up out of the mist, a fearsome sight; the horse took one look and bolted with me trying to hang to the cart. The plane's brakes were squealing with a horrible moan which made the old mare run like hell with the cart all over the place. My father cursed when I brought the horse home in such a sweat. He wouldn't believe my explanation as he was convinced that no planes could have been flying in that fog.

There was a minor incident by the hedge bank beyond the Clanford end of the runway.

About 2 o'clock one summer night I was woken by a sound like a tin shed falling down. I opened my bedroom window, saw a torch waving and heard voices shouting. An Australian voice was telling someone what he thought of him, his ancestors right back to Adam, and his unmarried parents.

Next morning the story came out. A Wellington had landed long, overshot the runway and hit the hedge bank at quite a speed. The Australian rear gunner had thought 'This is it!' when they left the runway, rotated his turret and baled out just as the plane came to a stop. He then picked himself up, walked round to the front of the aircraft and loudly told the pilot what he thought of him and his flying ability.

Another Wellington crashed at the airfield and only the rear gunner got out. It had been shot up. It landed on the runway by Williams Wood and crashed into the brook behind the gun butts. Possibly the brakes had failed. Loads of ammo were

dumped in the brook. Later when we were clearing the stream
we found a shoe with part of a foot still inside.

One crash was on the middle of the runway after a raid one
afternoon. There was a bang and a great pall of smoke.

There was one incident with an Oxford but it was during
the Wellington days so it must have been a liaison aircraft. A
sergeant had learned to fly unofficially and was at the controls.
He accidentally retracted the undercarriage while taxying. The
flight lieutenant had to take the blame for the accident rather
than admit there had been an unauthorised pilot.

Groups of some very nasty German PoWs worked on the
farm. They wore battledress with a large orange patch.

The first twenty gliders arrived in a flock and came in at
all sorts of impossible angles. We watched one coming in
and realised he was too steep to level out and land safely. It
plonked onto the runway but the pilot survived.

Woodside Cottage, just across the runway from Clanford,
was occupied by Mr Wheeler, a gamekeeper on the Seighford
estate. One afternoon an Albemarle dropped its tow rope too
far over that side of the airfield. The rope wrapped round
the chimney and yanked the whole lot off the roof just as I
was coming home from school. Mr Wheeler was standing
outside, looking at the great hole in the corner of his house
and shouting 'That bloody fool has stuck a rope round my
chimney and pulled it off.'

There were twenty or thirty Horsas and a Waco Hadrian at
the back of our farm. My cousin climbed into one Horsa and
ran down to the tail end. The glider promptly tipped onto
its tail. The loading practice was for the pilots to get in first

*then the troops take their positions from the front to back
to keep the balance.*

*The Albemarles would be drawn up on the runway with their
gliders waiting on the extension beyond the road.*

*A USAAF Dakota crashed right beside Woodside Cottage in
1945. The undercarriage collapsed and it bellyflopped right
against the garden fence. The RAF lads went and nicked the
Bendix radios.*

*One day my sister and I, both in school uniform, arrived back
in time to see a lot of Lancasters turn off the runway on to
the perimeter-track towards the north-east. The back door
on one plane was open and about twenty heads visible. The
men waved, whistled and shouted at us. I found out later
that they were PoWs just landing back from Germany. We
were the first English children the men had seen after years
of captivity.*

*In 1946 an Oxford was practicing one-engine approaches and
overshoots. It overshot the side runway and flopped down
near a pit. The RAF cut the engines out and set fire to the rest
of the plane (there were plenty of others still on the airfield).
One airman was left on guard until the engines were removed
and he stopped the boys collecting souvenirs.*

10

GROUND WORK

Each airborne aircraft and crew depended on twenty or thirty people on the ground.

Wartime aircraft were not stored neatly in hangars when not in use. The threat of enemy air raids meant that the planes were spread far and wide around the airfield's perimeter. Each had its own concrete platform, the dispersal hard-standing, reached by a short extension off the perimeter-track. Here the planes were refuelled, re-armed and underwent routine maintenance and repair.

These far-flung workplaces were made a little more bearable for the groundcrew by the provision of small workshops, flight huts and latrines. And tea was delivered to them by van.

A pilot had the right to order any of the groundcrew who had just worked on his aircraft to accompany him on the test flight – quite an incentive to conscientious attention to the task in hand.

* * *

On one occasion I was asked if I would like a flip. I sat in the rear gun turret and I remember flying round the Wrekin.

* * *

As an AC1 Fitter I was often sent over from Hixon to Seighford to carry out repairs which required expertise beyond the average mechanic's skill. I often had to work throughout the night to prepare an aircraft – with no light other than my torch.

One task usually done at night was spraying dope. As the dope was very inflammable, the hangar had to be cleared of everyone except for the two or three groundcrew actually doing the work. Soon the air was thick with the smell of pear drops, and we had to drink a bottle of milk to combat the effect of the fumes. There were no protective masks in those days.

The cluster of hard-standings and maintenance huts designated as 'D' Flight were right beside the farm buildings of Clanford Hall. This was about as far as you could be from the main facilities at Seighford. *Everyone at the dispersal had a bike because of the distance to the cookhouse.*

I was stationed at Seighford from 1942 to 1944 as a LAC Flight Mechanic (air frame). I was on 'D' Flight. They were a great bunch of lads. We had a Donald Duck emblem on the back of our jerkins. The Flight was by the farmhouse; the main dispersal Nissen hut was adjacent to the small wood.

Happy days in the summer were spent sitting in the sun, watching circuits & bumps. The farmer had two very tall pear trees and he let some of us take a few pears which we collected in an engine sheet.

Sometimes the planes would run off the runway and get bogged down. It then became our job to get them back.

One day one of the Fordson tractors from the MT yard arrived at a dispersed aircraft but could not stop – it badly damaged the bomb bay doors.

There were of course other specialist trades working on the ground at the airfield.

I was a Corporal Radio/Wireless Mechanic. On arrival from RAF Peplow in February 1945 I was put to work in the Signals Section adjacent to the electrical station beside the Woodseaves road. Among other jobs I drove a Commer signals van or a motorcycle combination which was used to transport accumulators and other pieces of equipment around the airfield.

Roy Kay was stationed at Seighford from January 1943 to April 1945 and so served with all three RAF units based there during the war. He believed that this possibly unique record was due to him being a Corporal Wireless Mechanic trained on the Lorenz Standard Beam Approach system. There were so few RAF personnel trained in this line that he was retained to maintain the transmitter each time the units changed.

There was one occasion when his trade put him in a potentially lethal situation. *A Wellington was taking off when it slewed across the field and ended up in the hedge near the petrol installation. All the crew got out safely but left the generators for the WT sets running and the lights on. I went into the aircraft to disconnect the batteries. There was a strong smell of petrol fumes and I could see blue haloes around the instruments.*

I was very pleased when I had switched off and got outside again. Only when I was back in safety did I realise that the Wimpy was fully loaded with fuel, bombs and incendiaries.

A good deal of the driving at an RAF station was done by members of the Women's Auxiliary Air Force. *The 'Queen Bee' ruled the WAAFs with a rod of iron but there were plenty of rude gestures behind her back. The WAAFs were a motley crew, one or two a bit odd – and some of their language was terrible.*

There was time for romance: LAC Roy Taylor married a WAAF from the aerodrome, and Harry Jones, a member of the RAF Regiment, met his wife-to-be there in late 1942. She was an 18-year-old MT driver. *One of her tasks was driving the flare path wagon. It was not unusual having to*

85

move the flare paths to another runway because of a change of wind direction. This meant extinguishing and relighting each time.

Other duties included taking the ambulance to Stafford Infirmary or the RAF Cosford Hospital, or carrying prisoners from the PoW camp at Gnosall to their place of work. Male drivers were usually sent for the latter job but if the MT was short-staffed WAAFs were sent with a guard. They were always told they must never leave their vehicle or talk to the prisoners.

On any trip through Stafford they always had to call at the railway station in case any personnel were waiting there for transport back to camp.

The RAF Regiment, formed in February 1942, had a contingent at Seighford.

They wore Army khaki rather than Air Force blue. They were very highly disciplined – when they came on kitchen duties they used to stand to attention and slam down their heels to me although I was only an LAC.

✳   ✳   ✳

I was a member of the newly-formed RAF Regiment. My time at Seighford was taken up with route marches, cross-country runs and the rifle range on Cannock Chase. We were on one of our runs over the fields towards Stafford when we were confronted by a man on horseback, complete with riding breeches and whip. He demanded to know 'What the hell do you think you are doing on my land?' We just ignored him and kept on running.

It was usual for members of the RAF Regiment to be accommodated in an area separated from the rest of the station personnel. At Seighford this dispersed accommodation site lay beside the eastern stretch of the Woodseaves-Bridgeford road.

We had no mains water in our quarters and a bowser was used to fill the tank in the toilet block. The Elsan chemical toilets were changed daily and placed on a sanitary wagon which had already collected from other sites and was always driven very carefully!

Each morning we had to walk to the ablutions on the main site to wash before breakfast. There was always plenty of hot water thanks to the good work of the boilermen.

We had a mongrel dog for a mascot until the day he was grabbed by an aircrew and taken up for a flight. From that day on he would have nothing more to do with the Regiment and stayed with the aircrew. He flew whenever they could take him up.

There was one sad duty for the RAF personnel at the station: the burial of colleagues who were killed during their flying training. Some were laid to rest in the Stafford Borough Cemetery; others were transported to their home town.

Due to my height, I was often detailed for the burial or firing parties. These were at the Eccleshall Road Cemetery or when the flag-draped coffins were taken to the railway station and loaded onto trains.

The Air Ministry Works Directorate had been formed in the 1930s with the role of organizing the construction and maintenance of airfields.

After being invalided out of the Army, I was appointed to Seighford as one of the first Air Ministry 'Works & Bricks' staff to work there. I cycled there every day from my home in Stafford. I was a fitter's mate to a Londoner named Alf, who called himself 'Popeye'. We looked after the sewage system, steam plants, boilers and water pipes, and the petrol pumps. One day I had to climb the water tower. It was a horrible experience and I would have refused to do it again. It was also a hard job crawling down under some of the sewage pipes but at other times our work was quite leisurely.

I was very lucky to have spent the war at Seighford. It was a free and easy job, and nobody seemed to check up on us. The food was marvellous (we scrounged all we could) and the pay wasn't bad.

Some of the dirtiest tasks were given to former aircrew who had been assessed as having a 'lack of moral fibre'. *There were some lorry drivers carting coal. These were the lack of moral fibre cases whose badges had been stripped off and they were given all the hard menial jobs.*

It seems to be a paradoxical situation but enemy prisoners of war also worked at the airfield. There was an Italian camp at Gnosall; most of them worked on local farms but some came to the kitchens at Seighford.

I saw some Italians who were employed mainly on the more menial tasks such as in the ablutions, where they tended to congregate. There were also Germans who kept themselves apart from the others and preferred to work in the open. They seemed to be content doing physical work maintaining the airfield and buildings.

✜   ✜   ✜

I encountered a few little men, very squat, with slanting eyes, who spoke no English and were employed on cleaning duties. I got the impression they were from Mongolia.

✜   ✜   ✜

I was at Seighford from January to July 1945 after my unit in Holland was disbanded. I was put on the Crash Crew. When I arrived there were loads of Italian PoWs putting up Nissen huts or doing all sorts of other jobs.

I think we had a haunted hut by the runway. It was about February 1945 when fog clamped in and I slept in it one night with three others from the Crash Crew. It was only a small hut occasionally used by aircrew. All four of us woke up about 2 a.m. and saw faces on the ceiling – in ghostly colours. We went outside, visibility was still only about ten yards. We heard later that these faces had been seen previously. They were believed to have been from a Wimpy that crashed on the drome.

11

READY FOR THE ENEMY

RAF Seighford never came under enemy attack. Not directly – but there may have been at least one attempt to bomb it. There certainly was an incident at Worston, a mere mile and a half away to the north-east.

It was a moonlit night about 1942/43. We were living at Great Bridgeford. My father heard the drone of a German bomber and threw me under the stairs for shelter. I heard five or six bombs drop. The Germans had spotted the coloured lights on the railway lines between Worston and Shallowford.

The German crew might have thought the lights were on the airfield, or perhaps their intended target was three miles beyond Worston. *The German pilot was probably looking for the Royal Ordnance factory at Swynnerton when he saw the railway lights reflected in the river and let his bombs go. He hit the railway lines and the river but mainly trees. The rails were bent and a lot of tree branches cut off. Billy Howells was in a wooden hut just across the river and he lost his voice for several days due to shellshock.*

✻   ✻   ✻

I saw the craters and indulged in the usual boyhood pastime of collecting bits of shrapnel. The bombs had straddled the railway line near Worston Mill.

There is no doubt that Luftwaffe aircraft were spotted in the Seighford neighbourhood on several occasions.
My mother saw a German bomber, with its black crosses, fly very low over Walton Hurst. We heard later that day about the raid on the English Electric factory at Stafford.

✻   ✻   ✻

I saw a German aircraft, probably a Dornier, with its big black crosses. There had been a raid on Liverpool and it may have been looking for landmarks. It reached Stafford then turned back along the Crewe railway line. The guns at the Universal Grinding Wheel factory opened up and I remember the lines of tracer across the sky.

Various enemy missiles descended on the district during the war. A load of incendiaries fell on Ellenhall Park and two landmines dropped on Lower Knightley. One of these mines lifted all the roof tiles on a cowshed. Another landmine shook buildings near Norton Bridge. A line of high explosive bombs came down between Spurleybrook Farm and the village of Ellenhall. And a silk parachute was picked up at the back of the schoolmaster's house in Seighford itself after one of the incendiary raids.

Farmer Frederick Parrott was the chief Air Raid Warden for the neighbourhood. *The local people said he made more damn noise with his whistle than the enemy bombers did.*

The threat of air raids was still being taken seriously in 1944. The school logbook recorded on May 11 that the children's gas masks had been inspected and tested.

A warm welcome was waiting if German bombers had attacked RAF Seighford. Four machine gun posts were sited beside the perimeter-track between Hextall Covert and Five Lane Ends.

There was one design while we were constructing the gun pits which consisted of a large concrete pipe set vertically in the ground. This proved impractical – when the actual gun was mounted in the pipe there was no room for the gunner!

The RAF Regiment had charge of the anti-aircraft guns. *Around the Springtime of 1943 we were issued with Lewis guns (obsolete even then) and we manned the gun pits on the airfield during daylight hours. On one occasion someone had the bright idea of providing us with a sentry box for shelter in wet weather. I happened to be on duty when a corporal arrived with some of our lads to position the box. The gun pit had a diameter of about six feet. The corporal told the lads to place the shelter right on the rim of the pit. Then, following the amused looks of everyone else, he realised that the sentry box would be shot to pieces if the gun was fired!*

The threat of an attack by enemy paratroops could not be ignored. Seighford, like other wartime airfields, was equipped with a defence command bunker, the battle headquarters. Massively strong and well concealed, the bulk of this concrete building was below ground level with just a narrow observation slit visible above an earth-covered mound.

A well-planned reception would have awaited the paratroops if they had ever landed on the airfield. In June 1940 Prime Minister Winston Churchill declared *every man in RAF uniform ought to be armed with something – a rifle, a tommy gun, a pistol, a pike or mace, and everyone without exception should do at last one hour's drill and practice every day. Each airman should have his place in the defence scheme. It must be understood by all ranks that they are expected to fight and die in the defence of their airfield.*

The threat of invasion still lingered while RAF Seighford was being built. Even when the tide had turned and Allied forces were poised to cross the Channel, the protection of this Staffordshire site continued to be planned in great detail.

Enemy action was likely to take one of two forms: either an air raid to destroy the airfield or an assault by airborne troops to seize it. Defence against the former was the sole responsibility of the RAF but the local Home Guard would be mobilized to assist with the defeat of any enemy paratrooper landing.

The sheer size of the airfield made it impossible to guard every square yard of the site. The defence scheme was based on four defended localities around the station where designated personnel would patrol as soon as the alarm was sounded.

Seighford's Defence Scheme set out the scenario of what would have happened if the enemy had appeared. At Alert II stage the anti-aircraft guns were manned and the crews ordered to fire if:

1) markings on the aircraft proved it to be an enemy machine

2) the aircraft dropped bombs or opened fire

3) orders from the Control Tower to the aircraft had been disregarded

The personnel on specific defence duties collected their firearms and went to their assembly points. Skeleton patrols were detailed for the vital installations on a 'two hours on – two hours off' basis. The rest of the personnel returned to their normal duties but carried their firearms.

The state of readiness was increased when Alert I stage was reached. The patrols were doubled, and each of the defended localities manned by a Defence Flight unit consisting of an officer, four sergeants and thirty-five airmen armed with rifles or Sten guns. Their role was to *immediately engage and eliminate the enemy.* A support section armed with machine guns, rifles, Sten guns and grenades was to hunt out and dispose of enemy troops wherever needed.

The 14th Battalion Staffordshire Home Guard were assigned to assist in the defence of the RAF stations at Hixon, Wheaton Aston and Seighford. Their duty was to:

1) establish a cordon round the area where paratroop landings had taken place

2) attack and round up such enemy troops as possible

3) if the airfield was taken, retake it at all costs

Local sections of the Home Guard were handily based at Great Bridgeford village hall, Ranton House, Seighford Hall and Ellenhall.

Albert Anslow had moved to Seighford in 1938. In 1940 he answered the call for volunteers to form a force to oppose enemy parachutists. As a veteran of the First World War, he was duly appointed sergeant of the Seighford Home Guard and soon heavily involved in his new duties.

Seighford Hall was empty after Colonel Dobson's death and his family had left. Permission was given for the saddle room to be used as the Home Guard guardroom. It was soon full of Mills bombs, grenades and rifles – enough to blow up the whole village.

My patrol was on duty two nights a week. There were about thirty men in the platoon and we practiced our drill at the back of the Hall. Some of the farmhands marched with a distinct gait due to the years of walking behind the plough.

We guarded the airfield area for about a year until the arrival of the first RAF personnel. We had slit trenches placed all round the construction site. Initially we had little more than homemade weapons such as knife blades mounted on long metal tubes to oppose enemy landings.

We had many callouts at night from the area command hut at Bridgeford when strangers were seen in the Seighford area. On one occasion we even detained the Post Office keeper from Haughton – we knew who he was but we couldn't resist a bit of fun. On another night an RAF officer stopped at our guardhouse and ordered a full parade. Although we started to obey his order we soon realised that he was returning from a party and was as drunk as a lord.

The Home Guard units attended weapon firing and grenade throwing practice on Cannock Chase. There were also platoon exercises when the unit from the Universal Grinding Wheel factory at Doxey would try to attack the airfield. It was not unknown for the local boys to join in and tell one group where 'the enemy' was hiding.

Agricultural duties were not neglected. *Many members of the Ellenhall Home Guard went off duty at 5 a.m. to milk their cows.*

RAF Seighford was a fairly accessible station with the Woodseaves-Bridgeford road and the Clanford road running through it but security was tight.

The road to Clanford which crossed the runway was sealed off with locked gates and out of bounds; even the Home Guard needed permission for entry. All access was monitored by RAF personnel.

Even the Brown family at Clanford Hall needed passes to use this stretch of the road to get to or from their farm.

Authorised visitors on the airfield also had to mind their own business. *As the Air Ministry Land Officer, I was a regular visitor to the station but one of the first things I learnt as a wartime civil servant was not to exhibit any interest in anything I saw or heard in which I was not directly concerned. On every visit I had to report to either the Adjutant or the Admin Officer. However I became a more or less honorary member of the Officers Mess – they were a great crowd to work with and for.*

There were times when security was very real. *During one German invasion scare we (groundcrew) were issued with rifles and ammo and had to do guard duties round the aircraft dispersals.*

One particular night, while I was on patrol with another man, two officers attempted so-called sabotage of the aircraft to check our efficiency. My colleague shouted 'Halt, who goes there?' Not getting a response, he fired and wounded one of them in the leg.

The airfield was a natural focus of interest for the boys of the neighbourhood and they duly tested its security.

A gang of us lads would sneak round the peri-track and get chased off.

✻   ✻   ✻

One night I was coming back on my bike from Gnosall via Five Lane Ends and decided to take a shortcut along the west perimeter track. I must have triggered some sort of alarm for very soon afterwards I heard voices and saw torch beams searching for me. I hid in the grass and the torches passed me. I followed at a safe distance and finally got back to the road at the end of the runway.

✻   ✻   ✻

I once actually got inside a Wellington parked on the dispersal bay at the Hextall end of the airfield. The little ladder was against the fuselage and we climbed up for a very quick look inside. I saw the pilot's seat, the bombs, the rear turret with thousands of rounds of ammunition in belts for the Brownings. We then pedalled away furiously on our bikes, expecting to be shouted at or grabbed at any second.

A favourite schoolboy pastime during the wartime was collecting pieces of shrapnel as souvenirs of enemy bombing raids. For Seighford youngsters there was a source of 'finds' much closer to home. After the Wellington crashed into the brook near William's Wood, the RAF recovery team did not bother to clear everything from the scene. At least three local boys came across live bullets lying in the water.

We found loads of ammunition, .303 bullets etc., dumped in the brook – presumably totally illegally.

✻   ✻   ✻

Tons of ammo, thousands of rounds, from the crashed aircraft were thrown in the brook. We found at least 500 rounds.

Many of these live bullets were recycled to become highly entertaining, and even more highly dangerous, devices detonated by their new 'owners'.

Such activities were contrary to the advice the culprits had often been given. The Seighford school log book recorded one such session: *6th December 1944 – a member of the police force attended today to give a talk on the danger of touching strange objects found lying about. He showed typical bombs and grenades, and explained their use.*

The residents of Ranton were possibly in more danger during the war than they ever realised. *One morning an RAF armourer told me to go to the field next to the gun butts if I wanted to see some fun. A group of Air Training Corps cadets were coming for weapon firing practice and they were being given Sten guns. The Sten had a nasty habit of rising violently when fired and the armourer anticipated that the people of Ranton would be 'having bullets landing on their heads'. Sure enough the gun barrels started to climb and the bullets went hosing away over the butts towards the village.*

12

OFF DUTY

By 1941 the pre-war system of having all the hangars and living quarters handily placed on the main airfield was totally unsuitable – they would have made a nicely concentrated target for enemy attack. So parts of the requisitioned Seighford farmland were earmarked for 'distributed accommodation'.

There were privileges of rank in the domestic quarters as an officer was entitled to more floor space than a sergeant who in turn had more space than an airman. There was one individual at Seighford who must have lost track of where he should sleep. *Something went wrong with his records coming through – he was a sergeant one day, then a flight sergeant; a day or two later he was a warrant officer; another day or two and he moved into the Officers mess as a pilot officer.*

It wasn't a case of working twenty-four hours a day for the 30 OTU personnel. There was time off and a variety of ways to spend it – transport permitting.

There were the taxi rides back from Stafford (after the pubs had shut, of course) with one of us, usually the air gunner, lying on the floor in the back whilst the rest of the crew rode in comfort.

Public transport was not an option at that time of night. A bus service ran right past the camp with a stop beside the main guardroom but the last bus back from Stafford left the town at 9 p.m.

I used to return from leave at my home in Croydon on the Euston-Crewe train. It didn't stop at Bridgeford so I had to get out at Norton Bridge at 4.45 a.m. and walk the six miles to camp. It never seemed a hardship as the countryside was really lovely.

*Seighford's station commander Wing Commander 'Robbie'
Roberts and his wife lodged at nearby Ellenhall*

There was entertainment at the station. ENSA shows and
concert parties were regular events, and there was also *a
lovely cinema*. By VE Day airfield security had relaxed and
local children used to pay threepence to watch the films
shown there.

The station's occupants took full advantage of their free
time.

A picturesque haven from the war:
Seighford Hall provided a stately YWCA hostel –
and a risk from the Home Guard arsenal!

We used to attend some damn good parties in the Officers
Mess.

✜   ✜   ✜

I remember the NAAFI: Corporal Dineage played the
accordion; a camp barber, who seemed elderly, did the sword
dance, and one chap, after a couple of free pints, would break
thick NAAFI plates over his head or stick pins through his
cheeks. But the beer usually ran out before things really got
out of hand.

✜   ✜   ✜

There were many good old parties.

✜   ✜   ✜

I did a few cross-country trips as a screened wireless operator
but my main job at Seighford was to do a daily inspection
of the wireless gear of about six Wellingtons. Once this was
completed my day was free. This led to my mate and I getting

on our bikes and taking off to the pubs, returning at night much the worse for wear.

*   *   *

We used to have an occasional dance held by the WAAFs.

*   *   *

Seighford Hall was used as a YWCA hostel for off-duty WAAFs. Men were allowed to visit but not to sleep there. However ...

*   *   *

We used to walk down from the camp to the YWCA in the Hall to listen to records. One of my favourites was Gigli singing The Lord's Prayer.

*   *   *

The first YWCA manageress was Mrs Jackson from Clitheroe. She was followed by Mrs Robertson. The Hall was also

Seighford Hall YWCA manageress Muriel White

*home to two Scotsmen, both RAF personnel. They had been
gardeners in civvy street and now tended the gardens and
grew some produce for the camp.*

Another refuge a short distance from the camp was Ellenhall
Vicarage. *The Reverend Richard Mears, the vicar of Ellenhall,
was the padre for RAF Seighford as the camp's living quarters
lay in his parish. He held an 'open house' on Wednesday
evenings when the airmen could play table tennis and have
cocoa. Some of the visitors were tense and forever smoking.*
The Holly Bush pub in Seighford village itself should have
been a natural attraction for the RAF personnel but it was not
too popular. *The old landlord restricted anyone in uniform
to just one pint of beer per visit.*

The pushbikes which transported so many of the groundcrew
across the wide open spaces of the airfield also had plenty of
use for social purposes.

There was the ride to Fox's shop in Great Bridgeford.

*   *   *

We used to cycle into Eccleshall of an evening for a drink.

*   *   *

*I remember one instructor called Steve, a sergeant with a very
posh public school accent. He was like a maniac when he had
had a few drinks. He jumped up and did Spanish dances on
the tabletop. He was eventually banned from all the pubs in
Eccleshall.*

*He was a navigator and they used to say you could give Steve
a penny pencil and a map from Woolworths and he could
take a kite over any town in Germany.*

*Coming back to camp one night after a boozing spree he found
a little pig in Great Bridgeford which he brought back to let
loose in the Aircrew Mess. But when he sobered up it turned
out to be a Jack Russell terrier dog.*

Another time when Steve and his mate, Paddy, were too far gone to walk back to camp they called at a farmhouse and asked the farmer if he could run them back in his car. He did so but then started thinking and phoned the police. The Home Guard and police were soon out looking for two 'German paratroops' who they thought had landed in the neighbourhood. Steve and Paddy were so frightened that they never set foot outside the camp for weeks after. We all knew who the culprits were but nobody let on.

A final 'Steve story'. After yet another boozing session, he was feeling so ill he sent Paddy to fetch a medical orderly. Full of sympathy for his great friend, Paddy took the opportunity to persuade the orderly to announce his diagnosis as a particularly nasty disease.

Beer was not the only attraction in the area. There were reputed to be 5,000 female munitions workers, *'The Lost Five Thousand'*, at the Royal Ordnance Factory at Swynnerton.

At Eccleshall we met the girls from the five hostels in the area who worked at the ordnance factories. They were allowed to invite us back on certain evenings for tea and cakes in their lounge.

Some encounters with the opposite sex were much nearer to base. *A cook sergeant had his own little room at the end of our Nissen hut. One night he managed to smuggle in a WAAF and sleep with her. The problem was getting her out again next morning before the orderly officer's inspection. It was daylight but she went out undetected in sidecar of a motorbike belonging to one of the maintenance workers.*

The sergeant had got away with it. For a time at least; the trouble was he couldn't resist bragging about his night of passion. Eventually the story reached the ears of his superiors and he was court martialled and reduced to the ranks.

The story has been independently confirmed – it was 'Popeye' of the 'Works & Bricks' team who smuggled out the WAAF in his sidecar.

Christmas did not pass uncelebrated. On one occasion Yuletide high spirits lead to an auxiliary petrol tank, which was shaped like a canoe, serving that very purpose on the duck pond near 'B' Flight.

The local residents benefitted socially from their temporary neighbours. *The Air Force band used to go round the villages, and played in the schools and village halls.*

Individual RAF personnel also became involved in the community. *The 1st Seighford Scout troop had a scoutmaster called Roland Jones. He was an air gunner and with us for a few weeks until he was lost over Germany. The leadership of the troop was then taken over by an Essexman, AC1 Jocelyn.*

AC1 Jocelyn in his role as Seighford scoutmaster

One groundcrew member went off duty unofficially – *I asked for leave when my son was born but it was refused because mother and baby were reported fine. So I went absent without leave and got fourteen days – but it was worth it.*

Another was off duty involuntarily – *I contracted diptheria, had a terrible throat on fire and was taken to the sick bay, then on to Stafford's isolation hospital. The medics at Seighford were ordered to fumigate the whole of my billet, which they did. But it turned out they had done the wrong hut and the blokes in it went raving mad!*

13

AFTER THE WAR

The war had scarcely ended when thoughts were given to the airfield's future. RAF records show that Air Ministry personnel visited the station on 23 August 1945 to attend a practice run by the RAC in connection with the use of Seighford for motor racing purposes. Nothing came of the idea and there would be no Seighford Grand Prix.

In October 1946, the Staffordshire Mental Hospital Board announced that it had decided to negotiate for the acquisition of the wartime airfield as the site for a replacement mental hospital. Four hundred acres were needed for the hospital and its own farm. In the end the negotiations fell through.

In due course the camp did acquire a new role when it became a 'temporary' home for Polish refugees. This lasted until the 1960s. Eventually the dozens of billet huts in the communal accommodation areas were dismantled and no trace remains of their existence.

Although 21 (P)AFU and its Oxfords had left by December 1946, the RAF did not finally abandon Seighford until 31 July 1947 when the airfield was declared to be a 'surplus inactive station'. It retained this status until 30 September 1950 when it was transferred to the Ministry of Aviation.

The 1950s began with the site empty and deserted. Then came a curious set of incidents that, for a time, put the area into the headlines. The story began on 25 June 1954 when the vicar of Seighford, with his wife and son, watched a large unidentified flying object moving silently backwards and forwards. At least eleven more 'flying saucer' incidents were witnessed in the Stafford area during the next six months. The occupants of a farm cottage at Ranton were terrified one

October afternoon when *a domed UFO* hovered over them before flying away at tremendous speed. Around the same time several people in Wolverhampton saw something streak across the sky from the Stafford direction.

The dozen incidents so intrigued author Gavin Gibbons that he made a detailed study of the reports. He plotted the routes of the mysterious objects and found the main sightings crossed over one small area – between Seighford and Ranton. Anxious to see the spot for himself, he cycled to the map reference and *pulled up suddenly when the road reached a wide, open space where rusty barbed wire was still to be seen. It was an aerodrome! The runways deteriorating and the administrative buildings long since deserted by the RAF personnel, it was a forlorn sight but, in spite of all this, an ideal spot for a landing.*

Gibbons wrote about the strange events in his book 'The Coming of the Spaceships'. He drew the conclusion that spacecraft had been carrying out reconnaissance missions in readiness for mass-landings at suitable sites on Earth – *it will not happen yet: perhaps not for several years.*

Half a century has passed and there have been no visitors from Space. His ominous predictions may have been fantasy but the basic question remains – just what did all those independent witnesses see in the local sky during those six months in 1954?

Conventional aircraft had not done with Seighford and the airfield gained a new lease of life in 1956. The Boulton Paul Aircraft Company had been contracted by the English Electric Company to carry out design modifications on the Canberra light bomber. The project was based at Boulton Paul's works at Wolverhampton but a site was needed for flight-testing. Seighford appeared to be suitable and a de Havilland Vampire was flown in to check. The Jet Age had arrived – with a vengeance as the blast from the Vampire's engine promptly blew the surface off the ageing runway. Resurfacing work soon took care of the problem and the airfield was back on the aviation map.

There was one other change. To meet the needs of their project, Boulton Paul built a third hangar between the existing wartime pair. It soon became quite a common sight to see the jets losing height and making their final approach below the surrounding treetops. Many of the Canberras were there for conversion work before going on to serve with foreign air forces including those of New Zealand, India and Sweden.

An unusual sight often seen outside the hangars in those days was a Tay Viscount jet airliner. This flying test-bed, fitted with electric signalling to its control surfaces, became the world's first 'fly by wire' aircraft. Boulton Paul's chief test pilot, A E 'Ben' Gunn, accordingly became the first pilot to fly by wire on all three surfaces. Following a wartime career flying Spitfires and Tempests, Gunn had moved into test flying at RAF Farnborough. He finally retired in 1971 after 17 years with Boulton Paul.

Experimental Seighford:
The Tay Viscount flying test-bed in 1960

There was at least one incident that brought back wartime memories for the local residents. On 1 January 1959 a Canberra had to make an emergency landing at Seighford. Ben Gunn was at the controls when the aircraft suffered total hydraulic failure as it took off. Before he could attempt a potentially dangerous landing, Gunn had to circle the area for a considerable time to use up his fuel. He eventually made a successful touch down with no flaps, brakes or nosewheel and the main undercarriage only half down. The Canberra overshot the Clanford end of the runway and was still

Famed as much locally for his driving as his flying, Boulton Paul's chief test pilot 'Ben' Gunn

moving when the boundary hedge arrived. He finally brought the plane to a halt without any damage apart from that caused by the collision with a large tree stump. Ben Gunn then departed to the Holly Bush pub to celebrate his safe return and the remainder of New Year's Day.

The potential disaster had brought out the emergency services. The airfield's own fire tender waited at the control tower end of the runway while the Clanford end was patrolled by a crew from the Stafford Fire Service. The latter team moved swiftly into action as soon as the Canberra landed, only to have their tender sink into a pit. It was several days before it was recovered from the mud.

Ben Gunn gained quite a reputation during Boulton Paul's occupation of Seighford, which he regarded as "a plum site", and duly passed into local folklore. He flew fast aircraft and is reputed to have tried to reach similar speeds in his car along Seighford's country lanes. This popular character, who died in 1999, still crops up in conversation when the airfield is mentioned.

Celebrities visited the airfield during those days. It was the scene of an historic meeting between Aviation Minister Roy Jenkins and his French counterpart to discuss the development of Concorde; and several members of the Royal Family met an aircraft of the Queen's Flight there while travelling to or from the Midlands.

The final military plane to use the Seighford runway was English Electric's supersonic fighter, the Lightning. With a maximum speed in excess of 1,500 mph, this was a world away from the Wellingtons, Albemarles and Oxfords.

Boulton Paul's contract with English Electric duly came to an end and the test-flight centre was no longer needed. They closed their Seighford operation in January 1966.

This departure raised the question once again of what next for the airfield. Various ideas were mooted over the years including a scheme for two prisons, one being a maximum security establishment. The most ambitious proposal was the idea of a civic airport for the city of Stoke-on-Trent. This might be seen as a fitting progression for the site but it received enormous opposition from the local residents. There were protest meetings, tractor drives and banners which left no doubt what the inhabitants of Seighford and Ranton wanted. The village hall at Great Bridgeford, once headquarters of the Home Guard, again helped to defend the countryside by hosting the public enquiry into the proposed airport. The local people won the day, despite having to face top barristers, when Major Eld referred to his right to the option of re-purchasing the land requisitioned from him during the War. So it was victory to the people of Seighford, and their landscape finally returned to peaceful farmland.

Soon after the enquiry ended most of the surviving runways were ripped out. It was noted that the wartime work, resurfaced by Boulton Paul, was *a hell of a job to get up*. This demolition effectively prevented the threat of large aircraft using the site. Just enough runway was left to allow light aircraft to take off and land. The former wartime airfield has accordingly provided many years of peacetime leisure flying.

One less popular activity took place in the 1980s. A parachuting club had access to the site and a small plane would drone upwards until it had sufficient height for the skydivers to jump. Then it would land, pick up its next passengers and begin its lengthy climb all over again. The noise of this operation annoyed so many local residents that the club was ultimately restricted to a maximum number of sessions per year.

The latest users of the airfield are much quieter. The Staffordshire Gliding Club was previously based high on the Moorlands beyond Leek. In 1992 they moved their headquarters to the ready-made landing ground at Seighford. Now single and double seater gliders soar gracefully above the old RAF station. Quite a contrast to the giant Horsas and Hadrians of 23 Heavy Glider Conversion Unit but a fitting link to round off the airfield's story.

14

COMMEMORATION

There's nothing to see at Seighford
There isn't a bridge of size
There's nothing at all unusual
And little to cause surprise

There's only a plain brick church
And the usual country inn
Where one hears music and laughter
And tales that countrymen spin

But those who have feasted on wonders
Turn to the simple and plain
And I, when tired of turmoil,
Shall come back to Seighford again

This poem was written by Sergeant Harold Adshead of RAF Seighford. Other ex-Air Force servicemen also remember the station with affection:

I was one of the first airmen to be posted to Seighford in 1942. I had done a tour of duty in Iceland and was posted to Hixon for a few weeks before going to Seighford as a chef and butcher in the Aircrew Mess, It was the best and happiest two years of my six years RAF service.

        ✳   ✳   ✳

My time at Seighford was as happy as one could expect in wartime, and I left with many pleasant memories.

        ✳   ✳   ✳

Aircrew huts in the edge of the airfield, 1992

I was serving as an Armourer in Holland until my unit was disbanded in January 1945. I was then posted to Seighford for six months – it was a smashing unit.

Their old aerodrome is still recognisable although most of it has reverted to farmland. Back in 1941 the Air Ministry regarded the actual airfield as the main priority; the buildings were only to be 'for temporary use'. Age, not surprisingly, has caught up with the few huts that survive and most of them look rather forlorn. Most of the features have disappeared altogether and the others may not survive much longer. For now, however, they create a lonely reminder of the wartime years.

The control tower, probably the most evocative relic on the airfield, remains although unsafe for use. What a fine facility it would have made for the Gliding Club. The majority of the remaining buildings lie between the tower and the hangars.

Many of the RAF buildings have disappeared or are just traceable by their foundations

Others are more remote, such as 'D' Flight's maintenance and small arms ammunition buildings where Bill Brown played as a boy.

Seighford Hall, once the YWCA accommodation and Home Guard base, has had a chequered history since the war. From 1947 to the mid-1950s it served as a training centre for Staffordshire Police's driving school. Then followed a spell when it was empty and almost derelict. The 'Swinging 60s' saw the transformation into Blazes Night Club and a hotel. Later it functioned a little more sedately as a retirement home for the elderly.

There is another physical reminder of wartime Seighford. A sad reminder of the price in human lives paid by the training units who used the airfield, and by the squadrons to which the trainees were posted. Just inside the main gates of the Stafford Borough Cemetery on the Eccleshall Road are two rows of military headstones. They include a dozen that bear the Royal Air Force badge. These simple stones are a mute testament to the tragic side of the Seighford story and the personnel who made the supreme sacrifice. This is the last resting place of several of the young men who died flying with 30 Operational Training Unit:

> pilot Adrian Beare and air bomber John Middleton, killed near Newbuildings Farm, Blithfield on 7 July 1943
>
> air gunners Eric Dean and Thomas Joyce who died at Hoar Cross on 29 December 1943
>
> air bomber Charles Yates, killed at Ranton on 24 February 1944
>
> pilot Spencer Cochrane and wireless operator Frank Powis, killed in the mid-air collision over Seighford airfield on 11 August 1944
>
> air gunner Leonard Meadows who died near Eccleshall on 8 January 1945

There has been a special act of remembrance. The Royal Air Force returned to Seighford for two days in 1993. This time it was in the form of a Gazelle helicopter which landed on the school playingfield. At 10 o'clock on that morning of Saturday 24 April the school gates opened to admit the public to an exhibition commemorating the fiftieth anniversary of the airfield.

The visitors included local families: youngsters to whom World War II was merely a topic in their history lessons; their parents; and their grandparents for whom the exhibits brought back memories of the village half a century earlier. And there were very special visitors from further afield – the veterans whose war service included a spell at RAF Seighford. There

Permanent reminders:
the two rows of headstones in
Stafford's Eccleshall Road cemetery

were groundcrew and aircrew. Happily there were those who had survived night raids in Lancasters; survived ditching in a dinghy on the North Sea; survived PoW camps after baling out over Germany.

Trips over the airfield in a civilian helicopter, or round it in a mini-bus, renewed their acquaintance with the station they had known from an OTU Wellington or a (P)AFU Oxford. There was the emotion of a pilot instructor on seeing the runway for the first time in forty-eight years: *Suddenly, for a few moments, I was back getting a green from the caravan at the end of the runway, pushing open the throttles and seeing the runway lights flash by and be left behind.*

And an air gunner: *I took a couple of trips in the helicopter and was allowed to sit alongside the pilot. Only having Perspex between me and the outside world, coupled with the throb of the engine, I felt as if I was back in the rear turret of a Wimpy again. I was amazed at how much of the terrain was still familiar.*

The idea for the weekend had begun a few months earlier when Staffordian Brian Podmore, noting various other wartime anniversaries being organised, thought it would be appropriate to commemorate Seighford airfield's service. Other enthusiasts were drawn in as the plans progressed. The focal point for the project was the exhibition in the village school (curiously though the committee's planning meetings were usually held in the Holly Bush!).

Their efforts fell into place and the event was opened by John O'Leary, the Chairman of Staffordshire County Council. The swarm of visitors enjoyed the assorted array of wartime memorabilia, vintage vehicles, and associated projects. The modern RAF was well represented as, in addition to the Gazelle helicopter, they provided displays by the Tactical Supply Wing and the Mountain Rescue Team from 16 MU at Stafford.

The highlight for many came during the Sunday afternoon. Scores of villagers and visitors thronged the pavements and eyes searched the sky. Growing expectation was rewarded by a special sight: the arrival of a Spitfire. The immortal aircraft made several passes over Seighford and the surrounding countryside.

The second day's programme also included an event that summed up the purpose of the project: a commemorative service in St Chad's parish church. The fifty years were spanned by the presence in the congregation of British Legion standard-bearers and RAF cadets. The service closed with the blessing and dedication of a plaque on the wall of the church porch. The wording on the plaque expressed, quite simply, the aim of the weekend's organisers:

SEIGHFORD AIRFIELD
1942-46

Dedicated to all Service and Civilian staff
stationed here during World War II
Many of whom gave their lives during the conflict

LEST WE FORGET

30 OTU
23 HGCU
21 (P)AFU

Long may they and their airfield be remembered ...

ACKNOWLEDGEMENTS

This book could not have been written without the help and interest of many people. They include:

Albert Anslow, Dennis Anslow, David Bate, Don Bayliss, Peter Bishop, Walter Carter, John Cooper, Mr T A Evans, John Foden, Charles Greaves, John Harris, Mr C V Hardy, Mrs Daisy Harvey, John Higginson, Ken Hughes, Harry Jones, Roy Kay, Brian Podmore, Basil Shillaker, Mr M P Smith, David Sparey, John Stubbs, Roy Taylor, John Teasdale, Peter Warrilow, Eddy Waters, Frank Young, and all those who responded to my appeal for information about the Wellington crash at Huntington.

Special thanks go to Reg White for his extensive recollections and thoughts as a Rear Gunner who flew from Seighford, and to Bill Brown for all his memories and hospitality (and his permission for me to spend many happy hours prowling around the airfield).

Grateful appreciation also goes to the Royal Air Force Museum at Hendon, and to Richard Robinson for his work at the Public Records Office, Kew. Last but never least my gratitude to Sheila for all her patience and understanding throughout the years it has taken this book to get airborne.

BIBLIOGRAPHY

Action Stations – Military Airfields of Wales and the
North-West
David J.Smith (Patrick Stephens Ltd)

Bomber Command Handbook 1939-45
Jonathan Falconer (Sutton Publishing)

Britain's Military Airfields 1939-45
David J. Smith (Patrick Stephens Ltd)

RAF Bomber Airfields of World War 2
Jonathan Falconer (Ian Allan)

RAF Bomber Command Losses volume 7 –
Operational Training Units 1940-1947
W.R.Chorley (Midland Publishing)

Staffordshire and Black Country Airfields
Alec Brew (Tempus Publishing Ltd)

The Six-Year Offensive
Ken Delve and Peter Jacobs (Arms and Armour)